D0908151

When the Red Sox Ruled

When the Red Sox Ruled

Baseball's First Dynasty, 1912–1918

Thomas J. Whalen

IVAN R. DEE
Chicago

Published by Rowman & Littlefield Publishers, Inc.
A wholly owned subsidiary of The Rowman & Littlefield Publishing Group, Inc.
4501 Forbes Boulevard, Suite 200, Lanham, Maryland 20706
http://www.rowmanlittlefield.com

Estover Road, Plymouth PL6 7PY, United Kingdom

Distributed by National Book Network

www.ivanrdee.com

Library of Congress Cataloging-in-Publication Data:

Whalen, Thomas J.
  When the Red Sox ruled : baseball's first dynasty, 1912–1918 / Thomas J. Whalen.
      p. cm.
  Includes bibliographical references.
  ISBN 978-1-56663-745-9 (cloth : alk. paper) — ISBN 978-1-56663-902-6 (electronic)
   1. Boston Red Sox (Baseball team)—History—20th century. I. Title.
  GV875.B62W53 2011
  796.357′640974461—dc22   2010048052

In loving memory of MaryAnne Whalen Spinale, 1928–2008

CONTENTS

PREFACE

The sports equivalent to hell freezing over occurred on the night of October 26, 2004. The Boston Red Sox, long the bridesmaid of professional baseball, managed to put aside eighty-six years of heartbreaking loss and humiliation by completing a four-game sweep of the St. Louis Cardinals in the World Series, thereupon becoming champions for the first time since Woodrow Wilson occupied the Oval Office. In the delirious champagne-soaked Boston clubhouse afterward, twenty-one-game winner Curt Schilling proclaimed that the club was "the greatest Red Sox team in history."

Given the dramatic nature of his team's victory, Schilling's exuberance is understandable, if somewhat misplaced. The 2004 Red Sox were a good team, a very good team, but hardly in the same class as their Fenway forebears of 1912–1918. For this earlier Beantown edition bestrode the narrow world of major league baseball like a colossus, capturing four World Series titles in seven seasons.

Blessed with Hall of Fame performers like Babe Ruth, Tris Speaker, and Harry Hooper, and near greats like Smokey Joe Wood, Duffy Lewis, Larry Gardner, Jack Barry, and Carl Mays, the Sox were easily the most dominant club of the Deadball Era, a period that ran roughly from 1900 to 1919 and was so named due to the softer composition of the ball used in competition. "Hitters couldn't drive the ball very far, and one run was often the difference between victory and defeat," noted the historian John M. Rosenburg. But this sobering reality did not seem to deter the Sox.

Outside of the lordly New York Yankees of 1936–1943, 1947–1953, 1956–1962, and 1996–2000, who won four or more championships apiece within a similar time frame, no other ball club in the twentieth century or beyond has surpassed Boston's run of sustained excellence.

"We won the American League pennant in 1912, '15, '16, and '18, and in between we finished second twice," said outfielder Harry Hooper, a major contributor to the team's success. "They never did beat us in the World Series. Never. We played four different National League teams in four different World Series and only one of them even came close. . . . The best team in baseball for close to a decade!"

How the Red Sox were able to accomplish this unique feat is the subject of this book. Like all tales of heroic accomplishment, however, it is best to start at the very beginning.

ACKNOWLEDGMENTS

In finishing this book, I am sadly reminded of two family members who will not get the opportunity to enjoy it: my late mother, MaryAnne Whalen Spinale, and my late uncle, James J. Fitzgerald.

My mom was my biggest booster and without a doubt exercised the greatest positive influence on my life. Her uproarious sense of humor and zest for living still bring warm memories. I can't thank her enough for all the unqualified love and support she provided. I'm sure she is up there in Paradise along with my late father, Herman T. Whalen, and late stepfather, Joseph D. Spinale, having a grand ole time singing among the celestial choir.

Uncle Jimmy was a member of "the Greatest Generation" who served his country faithfully and well during the Second World War. A quiet and dignified man, he moved through life with an effortless grace. He will be greatly missed.

As always, Dan Hammond and Christopher Callely bucked up my spirits when I needed it the most. They are the embodiment of what true friendship is all about. Ditto for Don Clemenzi and Steve Blumenkrantz, who provided welcomed encouragement and strength. Former Harvard Crimson star outfielder Elizabeth Crowley came through in the clutch, offering insightful comments and invaluable advice on improving the manuscript. She has my deepest respect and admiration.

Brian Walsh did a superb job as my research assistant. I wish him well in his new academic career. Thanks also to Fred Hammond, my old high school coach and history mentor who continues to inspire.

A special debt of gratitude is owed to the staffs of the Baseball Hall of Fame, the Holy Cross Archives, and the Boston Public Library. Their assistance and professionalism are greatly valued. Fellow Bates grad and baseball fanatic Chris Fahy earns a special mention for his unflagging enthusiasm for the project. Jon Sisk, Darcy Evans, and Ivan R. Dee did a marvelous job of getting the book ready for publication. They are true pros.

Others to single out for strong praise are Mary Alston-Hammond, Scott Ferrara, Wayne Ferrari, Joseph and Kristin King, Bob Connors, Pat and Hillori Connors, Laureen Fitzgerald, Gayle Clemenzi, Jodi Blumenkrantz, Tom Testa, Joseph and Theresa Dever, Linda Wells, Jay Corrin, Jim Dutton, Barbara Storella, Ben Varat, Jean Dunlavy, Edward Rafferty, June Grasso, Maureen Foley-Reese, Michael Kort, Shelly Hawks, Mary Ducharme, Tracey Nickerson, Matt Dursin, Matt Hallgren, Naomi Lomba-Gomes, John Mackey, Bill Tilchin, and Robert Wexelblatt.

Finally, I would be remiss if I didn't mention Teddy, my feisty and mischievous Siamese cat who left this world all too soon. She never failed to put a smile on my face and I will never forget her.

THE CRADLE OF BASEBALL (1871–1911)

On a December day in 1912, an otherwise staid gathering of uppercrust concert-goers at Boston's famed Symphony Hall were aroused from their torpor by the sight of Isabella Stewart Gardner entering the building. The elderly yet flamboyant Gardner, widely acknowledged as the city's first "Patroness of the Arts," was sporting a white headband emblazoned with the legend "Oh you Red Sox" in red letters. According to one local wag, "It looked as if the woman had gone crazy . . . almost causing a panic among those in the audience who discovered the ornamentation, and even for a moment upsetting [the orchestra] so that their startled eyes wandered from their music stands."

The august assemblage need not have registered such shock and consternation. Since its shadowy origins in the early days of the nineteenth century, the game of baseball had always held a unique appeal to Bostonians, even those with the advanced social pedigree of Gardner. Pitching great Albert Goodwill Spalding later put it best when he said "[j]ust as Boston was the cradle of liberty for the Nation, so also was it the cradle in which the infant game was helped to a healthy maturity." Indeed, it was in Boston that the first full-fledged dynasty in baseball history was born: the Red Stockings of 1871–1875.

The ball club itself was a carryover from the old Cincinnati Red Stockings, baseball's first professional team. Under the leadership of legendary player-manager Harry Wright, "the father of professional ball playing," the team strung together eighty-seven consecutive victories between 1869 and 1870.

As the story goes, wealthy Boston businessman Ivers Whitney Adams had become enamored of Wright's nine after they trounced several top local teams during a visit to the Hub in 1870. Looking to bring the same kind of unalloyed success to his hometown, Adams was able to financially induce Wright and a number of his teammates to relocate to Boston when Cincinnati disbanded at the end of the season. Adams even managed to commandeer the name "Red Stockings" for his new enterprise.

Playing in the National Association of Professional Base Ball Players (NAPBBP), a loose confederation of ten professional clubs that was founded in New York City in 1871, the Red Stockings dominated all competition. They finished a close second their first season, but breezed to the next four NAPBBP pennants.

Largely responsible for Boston's triumphal showing was ace hurler Albert Goodwill Spalding, an Illinois farmer's son who recorded a phenomenal 186–43 mark during the championship run. "In judgment, command of the ball, pluck, endurance, and nerve, in his position he has no superior," apprised early baseball chronicler Henry Chadwick. "His forte in delivery is the success with which he disguises a change of pace from swift to medium, a great essential in successful pitching."

Boston's perch atop the standings would come to an abrupt end after the 1875 season when Spalding and teammates Ross Barnes, Cal McVey, and Jim White bolted to the Chicago White Stockings. All Barnes had done was hit over .400 in 1872 and 1873, while McVey and White had proven their worth as steady run producers.

Aside from the lure of a higher salary, Spalding claimed he made the switch because Chicago owner William H. Hulbert had appealed to his sense of regional pride. "Spalding," Hulbert reportedly told him, "you've no business playing in Boston; you're a Western boy, and you belong right here."

In reality, the Machiavellian Hulbert had something far craftier up his sleeve. Convinced that his provocative action would invite condemnation from the NAPBBP, Hulbert resolved, in the words of the historian Geoffrey C. Ward, "to render them irrelevant by establishing a new league, with himself at the helm." And this is exactly what happened.

In a stunning coup d'etat, Hulbert was able to convince the presidents of four other NAPBBP clubs to join him at the Grand Central Hotel in downtown Manhattan to launch the National League (NL) on February 2, 1876. "There have been other forceful men at the head of our national organizations, men of high purpose, good judgment and fine executive ability," Spalding recalled admiringly. "But in all the history of Base Ball no man has yet appeared who possessed in combination more of the essential attributes of a great leader and organizer of men than did William A. Hulbert."

As a result, the NAPBBP ceased to exist. Finding the prospect of being on the outside looking in competitively disadvantageous, if not financially ruinous, Boston shrewdly opted to become a charter member of Hulbert's new league. However, with the exit of Spalding and his fellow "Seceders," the Red Stockings fell short of the standard of excellence they had set in the NAPBBP.

"The transfer of the Seceders meant first place for Chicago in 1876, fourth place for Boston," the journalist and historian Harold Kaese wrote. "Loyal Boston rooters would gladly have seen Hulbert's scalp blowing like a pennant from the wigwam of one of Sitting Bull's braves." This grisly sentiment notwithstanding, the Red Stockings' debut season in the NL was not a total loss.

George Wright, Harry's fleet-footed younger brother, batted a solid .299 and cemented his reputation as the game's premier shortstop. He "never had any equal as a fielder . . . he was really in a class by himself," said teammate and Hall of Fame catcher Jim O'Rourke.

Wright remained an important fixture on the NL champion Red Stocking teams of 1877 and 1878, which featured the outstanding pitching of Tommy Bond. A pioneer curveball specialist, Bond bobbed and weaved his way to forty victories both seasons, en route to becoming the first pitcher in NL history to reach the century mark in wins. Bond "was just the pitcher [Harry] Wright needed to help Boston return to its pennant-winning ways," wrote historian Gary Caruso.

Equally vital to Boston's resurgence was the arrival of new team president Arthur H. Soden. The Civil War veteran had made a fortune in the roofing industry and was quick to tell anyone willing to listen that he considered baseball a business. Period. To this end, he successfully lobbied other owners around the league to adopt the reserve clause, a far-reaching measure that, according to the writers Donald Dewey and Nicholas Acocella, "kept players bound to their clubs through an indefinite option year at the lapse of a specified contract."

For an entrepreneur like Soden it made perfect sense, given the high turnover rate that existed on team rosters during this period. "What man in his right mind will invest money in this business?" he asked. "Today he has some assets. Tomorrow he may have none."

Soden's reserve clause brought some much needed stability to the game, albeit at the expense of the players, who now found themselves reduced to "a state of high-salaried peonage." Save for the occasional challenge brought by a rival major league operator, this economic state of affairs remained in place until 1975, when an independent arbitrator named Peter Seitz overturned the reserve clause and ruled that owners had no right or power to retain a player's services "beyond the 'renewal year' in the contracts which these players had heretofore signed with their clubs."

When not focusing on the financial aspects of the game, Soden showed himself to be a fairly astute judge of talent. Under his regime, which ran from 1877 to 1906, Soden was able to bring in such future Hall of Famers as Charles "Kid" Nichols, Hugh Duffy, and Tommy McCarthy. The right-handed Nichols won 331 games while in a Boston uniform between 1890 and 1901 and could boast of having one of the liveliest fastballs on the circuit. His streak of seven consecutive thirty-win seasons between 1891 and 1897 still remains a major league record.

As for Duffy, the lanky center fielder batted an all-time best .440 in 1894 and dazzled fans with his uncanny ability to get on base. "He was a choke hitter who could rap hits everywhere with power," remembered one contemporary. Duffy teamed up with McCarthy, a .292 career batsman with a shotgun arm in right, to give Boston one of the better hitting outfield duos in baseball. Appropriately, they were called the "Heavenly Twins." With the influx of such proven stars, Boston went on to win pennants in 1891, 1892, 1893, 1897, and 1898, establishing itself as the NL's "team of the decade."

Not all of Soden's moves panned out, however. In 1887, he purchased outfielder and catcher Michael "King" Kelly from the Chicago White Stockings for a then record sum of $10,000. Arguably the greatest ball player of the nineteenth century, Kelly could do it all: run, hit, hit with power, throw, and catch. During his seven years with the White Stockings, the "King of Baseball" won batting titles in 1884 (.354) and 1886 (.388) while leading his team to five pennants.

But statistics alone do not convey the kind of stylish élan he exhibited on the playing field. "Once he stood on the base lines, his wide shoulders back, and a look of studied innocence on his face, the crowd had eyes for nothing else," noted the historian Robert Smith. Indeed, Kelly possessed great charisma, but he was not without his share of personal foibles.

An inveterate spender and drinker, Kelly got under the skin of many a manager. "Time and again I have heard him say that he would never be broke, but money slipped through Mike's fingers as water slips through the meshes of a fisherman's net, and he was as fond of whiskey as any representative of the Emerald Isle," complained Chicago skipper Cap Anson. When a journalist once boldly inquired as to whether he imbibed on the job, Kelly didn't miss a beat. "It depends on the length of the game," he answered.

Michael "King" Kelly: The controversial Boston star's antics both on and off the field endeared him to fans but alienated his teammates and manager. (Courtesy of the Library of Congress.)

While this puckish attitude may have endeared him to fans and writers alike, it did not produce any immediate championships for Boston. In fact, his "extravagant personality" became a major disruptive influence inside the clubhouse as many of his teammates came to regard Kelly as a selfish prima donna. It didn't help matters that Kelly locked horns with his manager, the popular John Morrill.

The feud got so bad that Morrill was forced to step down by team ownership, further dividing the roster. "It came down to who should go," Soden explained afterward. "Morrill has many friends in this city and is a perfect gentleman. Kelly is a ballplayer. So it was for us to choose between the men, and we picked out Kelly as the one who could win the most games."

For Soden's public display of support, Kelly rewarded him by jumping to the Boston Reds of the Player's League (PL) in 1890. Organized by the Brotherhood of Professional Baseball Players, the sport's first union, the PL was a direct challenge to the senior circuit's increasingly monopolistic hold on the game.

"All players were guaranteed salaries at least equal to what they made in 1889, as well as equal representation with the financiers on the League's board of directors," notes historian Charles Alexander. However, poor attendance and a lack of investment capital drove the league out of business after only one season of operation.

Undaunted, Kelly briefly rejoined Soden's club late in 1891 as a part-timer before leaving for good the following year. In the interim, he had kept himself active playing for the Cincinnati Porkers of the American Association (AA), yet another big-league competitor that the NL absorbed in 1892.

But at this juncture, Kelly had become a mere shadow of his former self as his dissolute behavior both on and off the baseball diamond had finally caught up with him. He would die of pneumonia at Boston City Hospital in 1895. He was only thirty-six.

When the twentieth century began, the once mighty Red Stockings, who now went by the name Beaneaters, were reduced to being a mediocre outfit. In fact, over the span of the next five decades, they would win only two more pennants before electing to leave Boston altogether for the greener pastures of Milwaukee in 1953.

Accounting for this sudden collapse were several factors: Soden's declining interest in the club, fading stars, and the emergence of a popular new rival that would supplant the Beaneaters in the hearts and minds of most Bostonians.

Called the Americans, this new team was the brainchild of Byron "Ban" Johnson, a former sportswriter turned baseball magnate. As president of the Western League, a minor circuit that operated out of such small midwestern cities as Grand Rapids, Kansas City, and Indianapolis in the 1890s, Johnson had long entertained thoughts of upgrading his property to major league status.

By 1901, he was able to turn his dream into reality with the establishment of the American League (AL). So named to give it, as the authors Bob Klapisch and Pete Van Wieren point out, "a more national character," the new loop was composed of eight teams, including franchises in major urban markets like Chicago, Detroit, Philadelphia, and Cleveland. "The American League will be the principal organization in the country within a very short time," Johnson vowed.

To make good on his pledge, Johnson persuaded AL owners to do whatever it took to sign established players off NL rosters, even if that meant offering higher salaries and lengthier contracts. "The move was successful," concludes historian John P. Rossi. "Although the figures vary, one source estimates that of 182 players of the American League during the 1901 season, 111 were former National Leaguers."

Interestingly enough, Johnson originally had no intention of putting a ball club in Boston, as it was then considered "a National League stronghold." But when the senior circuit actively tried to sabotage his efforts with the hollow threat of supporting a third league "to go head-to-head against the AL in most American League cities," an angry Johnson lashed back. He announced that there would be an American League team in Beantown after all.

The proud and pugnacious founder of the American League, Ban Johnson had big appetites and even bigger ambitions. (Courtesy of the Library of Congress.)

"The hostile attitude of the National League is responsible for us adding Boston," Johnson said.

Bankrolled by coal and timber baron Charles W. Somers, a Johnson business associate who was known to provide "emergency funds" to AL teams in need, the Americans made an immediate splash on the local baseball scene. They raided the Beaneaters of several of their top players, most notably Jimmy Collins.

A future Hall of Famer and lifetime .294 hitter, Collins was considered the slickest fielding third baseman of his generation. He was also a natural leader, as evidenced by his selection to become the team's first captain and field manager. He "was one of the fastest men ever to step on a baseball diamond," longtime Philadelphia Athletics manager Connie Mack praised. "He could hit to all fields and threw the ball like a jet-propelled rocket."

A Hall of Fame third baseman, Jimmy Collins led the upstart Boston Americans to consecutive league pennants and a World Series championship during his noteworthy tenure as player-manager. (Courtesy of the Boston Public Library Print Department, Sports Temples of Boston Collection.)

As for the efficacy of switching leagues, Collins personally voiced no regret, as his old salary of $2,400 per season with the Beaneaters was increased nearly two-fold. "I like to play baseball, but this is a business with me, and I can't be governed by sentiment," he explained. "I am looking out for James J. Collins."

Joining Collins on the Americans' roster was a portly right-handed fireballer by the name of Denton True "Cy" Young. Already well on his way to compiling the greatest number of victories in baseball history with 511, the thirty-four-year-old pitching ace came to Boston following an unhappy two-year stint with the St. Louis Perfectos of the NL.

Feeling underpaid and underappreciated by St. Louis management, Young wasted little time in signing with the Americans when Somers offered him a $4,000 contract. "It was all right for Cy to jump," a friend determined, "because if the league folded he wouldn't have any problem getting another job."

In his previous eleven years as a big leaguer, Young had averaged an outstanding twenty-six victories and 112 strikeouts per season. "When I would go to spring training, I would never touch a ball for three weeks. Just would do a lot of walking and running. I never did any unnecessary throwing. I figured the old arm had just so many throws in it, and there wasn't any use wasting them," he said of his success on the mound.

With Collins and Young plying their considerable skills on the baseball diamond, the Americans were able to capture second place in their inaugural AL campaign, a scant four games behind the pennant-winning Chicago White Sox. Of even greater importance, however, was that the team won the battle of the turnstiles.

Playing their home games at the recently opened Huntington Avenue Grounds near Symphony Hall in Boston's historic South End neighborhood, the Americans decisively outdrew the Beaneaters, 289,448 to 146,502. (Overall, AL attendance was a robust 1,683,584, just 236,000 shy of the NL's.)

CHAPTER ONE

Despite his advancing years, Cy Young was still the undisputed ace of the early Boston pitching staff. "I had a good arm and legs," he once said. (Courtesy of the Library of Congress.)

While part of the explanation for this turnabout lies in the superior on-the-field performance of the Americans (the Beaneaters had stumbled to a fifth-place finish with a 69–69 record), it doesn't tell the full story. "The new team in Boston was smart about its public relations, creating a 25-cent section in the bleachers and letting kids in for free," note Klapisch and Van Wieren.

In contrast, the unimaginative Beaneaters' ownership, well known for its penurious ways, charged a full fifty cents for bleacher admission and spurned the whole notion of letting anyone in for free. Whatever the underlying cause, the Americans had successfully demonstrated that they, like the upstart league they represented, were no joke. Indeed, they planned on sticking around for awhile.

After dropping to third place the following season, the club broke through with a 91–47 mark in 1903, good for the pennant and a fourteen-and-a-half-game lead over their nearest league competitor. Not surprisingly, Young was the main catalyst in the championship drive, as he notched a league-leading twenty-eight victories to go along with a sparkling .757 winning percentage.

"I was real fast, but what few batters knew was that I had two curves," Young later revealed. "One sailed in there as hard as a fastball and broke in reverse, and the other was a wide break. I had good control, too. I aimed to make the batter hit the ball, and I made as few pitches as possible."

Others making major contributions from the mound were Bill Dinneen and "Long" Tom Hughes, who registered twenty-one and twenty wins respectively. "When a team has pitching such as I have, it is bound to win a lot of games," Collins said.

Even so, the team was not devoid of offense. Leading the league in six major batting categories (batting average, hits, home runs, triples, slugging percentage, and runs), the Americans were a virtual wrecking crew. Sending the most fear into opposing pitching staffs was Patsy Dougherty, a second-year outfielder who paced the club with a .331 batting average. Fellow flycatcher Buck Freeman, who stood at a less than imposing five feet, nine inches, also lent a hand by cracking thirteen homers to lead the AL.

As for Collins, the flashy player-manager had another solid year at the plate with a .296 average and seventy-two RBIs. Yet it was his stellar glovework at third that continued to earn him the most plaudits. "The most difficult balls find their way into his hands as if by magic," a popular journal of the day, *Sporting Life*, marveled.

"Whether the bound was long or short, high or low, on one side or the other, or if it comes upon the most difficult pick-up imaginable, it can not escape him, and is never too quick to elude him. His plays back of the bag are wonderful, and his throws so strong that he can catch the fastest runner."

One figure not on hand to bask in the glow of the Americans' pennant-winning triumph was Charles W. Somers. Realizing that he "had been whirling too fast and loose with his assets," Somers decided to prudently sell the team before the start of the season to Henry J. Killilea, a Milwaukee attorney and Ban Johnson acolyte.

In January, Killilea had played a critical role in brokering a peace settlement between the AL and NL, which became known as the "National Agreement." In basic terms, the accord pledged that the two competing circuits would "co-exist peacefully" and "abstain from signing the other league's players."

In addition, the reserve clause would be retained. To ensure that these terms were properly enforced, a new three-man governing body for the sport was created called the "National Commission." Made up of Johnson, NL president Harry Pulliam, and Cincinnati Reds chief Garry Herrmann, who was selected by the owners of both leagues to act as chair, the commission was to rule the game "by its own decrees . . . answerable to no power outside its own."

While Herrmann technically held the most authority, it was Johnson who really called the shots. His fierce determination, domineering personality, and cunning intellect proved too much for his fellow commissioners to overcome. They meekly submitted to his will, making Johnson "the most powerful figure in baseball" over the next fifteen years, according to baseball historians Dewey and Acocella.

Killilea's skills as a negotiator would again prove instrumental near the close of the 1903 regular season. Barney Dreyfuss, the owner of the NL champion Pittsburgh Pirates, approached Killilea about the possibility of staging a playoff series between their respective clubs. "The time has come for the National League and American League to organize a World Series," Dreyfuss argued. "It is my belief that if our clubs played a series on a best-out-of-nine basis, we would create great interest in baseball, in our leagues, and in our players. I also believe it would be a financial success."

There was precedent for such a move. Between 1884 and 1892, the pennant winners of the NL and the old American Association had met regularly in a postseason series for the "Championship of the World." When the AA went belly up in 1892, the NL held its own interleague championship series called the "Temple Cup" for a number of years. Named after one-time Pittsburgh team president William Temple, who went to the trouble of providing the emblematic silver trophy, the series pitted the league's top two finishers on the regular season against one another in a best-of-seven format. But fading fan interest forced the series to be discontinued by the turn of the century.

Hoping for a more favorable response this time around, Killilea gave his assent to Dreyfuss's proposal after it was worked out between them that all World Series gate receipts would be evenly divided and that each team would "bear the expense of the games played on their respective grounds, excepting the expense of the umpire."

Yet more than money was at stake here. The credibility of the entire AL was on the line, because a victory, in the words of historian Donald Honig, "would dispel any lingering vestiges of doubt about its equality [to the NL]." Thus when Killilea first broached the idea to Johnson, the opportunistic AL boss asked, "Do you think you can beat them?" When Killilea answered in the affirmative, Johnson replied, "Then play them. By all means, play them."

Victory was no sure thing, however. The Pirates boasted a formidable array of hitting talent starting with slugging shortstop Honus Wagner. The "Flying Dutchman" was in the middle of a Hall of Fame career that would produce eight NL batting titles, 3,420 hits, and a lifetime .328 average. He "takes a long bat, stands well back from the plate and steps into the ball, poling it," assessed one impressed opponent.

Providing further punch to Pittsburgh's lineup were outfielders Ginger Beaumont and Fred Clarke, reliable .300 hitters who were equally adept at driving in runs. "I think we have it all over them," bragged Pirate third baseman Tommy Leach on the eve of the series. "I don't see how we can lose. I know the Boston Americans are in the upper class as a ball team, and nobody but a lunatic would deny that. Still, we have been playing together a long time. . . . The Boston Americans will realize that they are up against the toughest proposition yet when they stack up against Pittsburg. It will be a fight from the drop of the hat, and no doubt the better team will win the series."

To Leach and Pittsburgh's everlasting dismay, that better team turned out to be Boston. After falling behind three games to one, the Americans came roaring back to take the series with four straight wins. "While such a result was unlooked for by the loyal followers of the home team, and while their disappointment is consequently keen, the truth must be acknowledged that the National leaders were fairly and squarely outplayed," the *Pittsburg Dispatch* reported.

As had been the case all season for Boston, pitching proved to be the decisive factor. Young and Dinneen accounted for all five of the team's victories while collectively holding Pirate batters to under two runs a game. "It was the greatest thing for baseball known in years," the *Boston Herald* pronounced afterward.

Cheering the Americans on to victory were a particularly boisterous group of local fans known as the "Royal Rooters." Drawn mostly from the blue-collar ranks of Boston's teeming Irish-Catholic community, the over three hundred strong Rooters took their lead from a colorful local tavern owner named Michael "Nuf Ced" McGreevey.

Sporting a handlebar mustache and a stocky physical frame, this son of Irish immigrants regularly entertained patrons at his Columbus Avenue drinking establishment with a near encyclopedic knowledge of the game. Whenever a baseball argument broke out, which is to say all the time, he would invariably settle it with the terse rejoinder "nuf ced!"

The spiritual leader of Boston's famed Royal Rooters, Michael "Nuf
Ced" McGreevey and his fellow "cranks" serenaded the Pittsburgh
Pirates to the point of distraction with a spirited rendition of the song
"Tessie" during the 1903 World Series. (Courtesy of the Boston Public
Library Print Department, Michael T. McGreevey Collection.)

"He was a student of the game and a close friend of his era's
current and old-time stars," notes the writer Peter J. Nash. "He
had no love for the 'hanger on' prone to hero worship, who he
considered 'the worst pest in the family of fans.' He was an insider,
respected by the baseball fraternity, and a leader amongst the fans
he served at his 3rd Base saloon."

McGreevey wasn't a bad athlete either. An accomplished hand-
ball player and swimmer, he frequently was invited to don a Boston
uniform during spring training and take fielding practice. Once, a
minor league owner became so impressed with his glove work that

The Huntington Avenue Grounds was the Boston Americans' home park and site of baseball's first World Series in 1903. (Courtesy of the Boston Public Library Print Department, Sport Temples of Boston Collection.)

he offered the Boston management $300 for his services. Notified of the deal, McGreevey laughed it off. "I guess you have been handed a good sized lemon," he told the bewildered owner.

During the Series, McGreevey was in top form, exhorting his fellow "cranks" to serenade the Pirates with a spirited rendition of the song "Tessie" from the popular musical comedy *Silver Slipper*.

> Tessie, you make me feel so badly.
> Why don't you turn around.
> Tessie, you know I love you madly.
> Babe, my heart weighs about a pound.
> Don't blame me if I ever doubt you.
> Tessie, you are my only, only.

This nonstop refrain proved too much for some Pittsburgh players. "We laughed at first, but after a while it got on our nerves," claimed Leach. "They kept singing it over and over, and so damned loud. One of the fellows said, 'If I ever meet this gal Tessie, I'm going to punch her in the nose.'" The Americans were understandably more tolerant of the Rooters' shenanigans.

"The support given the team by the 'Royal Rooters' will never be forgotten," said Jimmy Collins. "They backed us up as only Bostonians could, and no little portion of our success is due to this self-same band of enthusiasts."

The Americans repeated as AL champions in 1904, but not before surviving one of the tightest pennant races in history. Led by right-hander Jack Chesbro, a spitballer who posted a major league record forty-one victories on the year, the New York Highlanders (later called the Yankees) fought the Americans tooth and nail down to the final day of the season, a scheduled doubleheader between the two clubs at New York's Hilltop Park.

Clinging to a one-and-a-half-game advantage in the standings, the Americans required only a split to take the flag. But New York had home field advantage and Chesbro. In the end, neither would prove to be enough. The Americans took the first game and the pennant when

Spirited displays of support from fans like this one gave the Americans a decided home field advantage in their 1903 championship showdown with the Pirates. (Courtesy of the Boston Public Library Print Department, Michael T. McGreevey Collection.)

a wild pitch by Chesbro in the ninth inning of a 2–2 tie allowed Boston base runner Lou Criger to score the winning run from third. "The players did it all," a relieved Collins declared afterward. "I had a great team of ballplayers to manage; they did everything I asked of them."

And no Boston player performed at a higher level than Cy Young. Once again leading the staff in wins (26), strikeouts (200), and ERA

(1.97), Young shouldered the bulk of the team's pitching load down the stretch. In games he started during the last four weeks of the season, the club reeled off an impressive 7–1 mark. "Without Cy Young's contributions in September and October," writes biographer Reed Browning, "the Boston Americans would have lost the pennant."

Adding further luster to his standout season was the perfect game he pitched against the Philadelphia Athletics on May 5, the first in the big leagues since 1880. "I don't think I ever had more stuff, and I fanned eight," Young said of his stellar outing before a hometown crowd of ten thousand spectators. "The closest the Athletics came to a hit was in the third when Monte Cross hit a pop fly that was dropping just back of the infield between first and second. [Buck] Freeman came tearing in like a deer from right and barely caught the ball."

Unfortunately for Young and his teammates, there would be no opportunity for further heroics that postseason. That's because John T. Brush, the mercurial owner of the NL champion New York Giants, refused to allow his club to play the Americans in the World Series. Brush had been incensed at Ban Johnson for placing an AL team in New York to directly compete against his Giants. His opting out of the Series then was his own way of getting even, despite charges in the media and among fans that he was acting in a cowardly manner. "All this ran off Mr. Brush like water off a duck's back," Giants manager John J. McGraw later said. "He was a man of great determination, firm as a stone wall."

Still, it could not have gone down well with Brush that a reputable national publication like the *Sporting News* proclaimed Boston "World Champions by default." Indeed, before the start of the 1905 season, Brush caved in to popular pressure and got owners in both leagues to agree to a new set of governing principles that required the "pennant-winning club of the National League and the pennant-winning club of the American League [to] meet annually in a series of games for the Professional Base Ball Championship of the World."

These rule changes must have brought little consolation to new Boston owner John I. Taylor, who had been denied the opportunity of reaping a financial windfall with the cancellation of the previous fall's World Series. Taylor liked making money almost as much as he liked spending it. But he had not always been so enterprising.

The twenty-nine-year-old son of *Boston Globe* publisher and Civil War veteran General Charles H. Taylor, "John I." had acquired a well-earned reputation around town as a screw-up, a spoiled kid who preferred frequenting the local bar scene to putting in an honest day's work. It was for this reason that his father fronted him the money to buy the Americans from Killilea for $145,000. The general hoped the purchase would spark the ember of ambition in his "wild son," as John I. had previously expressed a strong interest in baseball. Besides, it would give him "something to do."

Killilea was more than willing to go along with this arrangement as he had been looking to cash out after receiving a deluge of unfavorable press notices following Boston's Series triumph over Pittsburgh. Pirates owner Barney Dreyfuss had magnanimously given all his gate receipts to his players, while Killilea had conspicuously refused to do the same. For this alleged perfidy, he was publicly branded a "greedy cheat."

In taking over the reins of the ball club, Taylor promised not to rock the boat: "I have the utmost confidence in Jim Collins and consider him as good a manager as there is in the country, and shall co-operate with him so far as it lies in my power to give Boston as good ball as it has had in the past, and will spare neither money nor effort in that direction."

It did not take him long to break this pledge. A compulsive meddler with a hair-trigger temper, Taylor saw nothing wrong with entering the clubhouse after a tough loss and upbraiding his players for their perceived deficiencies.

"Somehow or other, he was acquainted with every skeleton in our closets," remembered catcher Bill Carrigan. "He knew as much about our night life as about our morning and afternoon activities." Such an authoritarian approach upset the ever prideful Collins, who took an instant disliking to his new boss. As one newspaper reported, Collins

John I. Taylor was the family screw-up and pampered rich kid who became team owner in 1904. "He had a damn good time and gave other people a damn good time," a descendant said. (Courtesy of the Boston Public Library Print Department, Sports Temples of Boston Collection.)

"has suffered a great deal of annoyance in the management of the affairs of the club through the activity displayed by John I. Taylor."

Taylor further inflamed the situation by making a series of ill-advised front office moves, including the trade of slugging left fielder Patsy Dougherty to the New York Highlanders for unheralded backup infielder Bob Unglaub, which the historian Howard Liss has deemed "unquestionably the worst deal" made by Boston in the pre–World War I era.

His patience finally exhausted, Collins stepped down as manager near the end of the 1906 season, a woeful campaign that saw the former World Series champs drop all the way to the AL cellar with a 49–105 mark. "There was never a dull moment when John I. was around," Carrigan said.

Things got only worse for Taylor and the club the following spring training. On March 28, star outfielder Chick Stahl, Collins's replacement as player-manager, committed suicide in his hotel room in West Baden Springs, Indiana. He died shortly after ingesting a bottle of carbolic acid. "My God," commented teammate Lou Criger, "I can't realize it yet, but thank goodness he did not suffer long. Stahl was a king among men. He was the squarest man I ever knew."

Square or not, accounts later surfaced that the recently betrothed Stahl had grown despondent over blackmail threats he had received from a Chicago woman with whom he had engaged in a romantic tryst. She claimed that Stahl had gotten her pregnant and reportedly was prepared to reveal this fact to the world if he rejected her offer of matrimony. Not knowing where to turn, a clearly overwrought Stahl decided to end it all. "I couldn't help it," he said before passing away.

With Stahl's untimely death, Taylor's immediate instinct was to name Cy Young the team's new player-manager. But the aging hurler politely turned him down. "Judging from the way I have been going this spring, I believe I will have my best year in base ball this year and I would rather not have anything to worry me," Young explained.

Disappointed, Taylor tried out former University of Illinois athletic director George Huff and Bob Unglaub in the dugout before finally settling on veteran catcher Deacon McGuire. It hardly mattered, as the Americans played under .500 ball, finishing in seventh place, forty-seven games behind Chicago.

As for Young, after posting two consecutive losing seasons, he returned to form with a 22–15 record. "That old fastball of his is about as effective as it ever was," observed teammate Bunk Congalton. "He uses his head, too, and has the faculty of making men play behind him."

By 1909, the team had begun to show signs of life again, winning eighty-eight games and staying in the thick of the pennant race for most of the season. Chiefly responsible for this revival was the emergence of young players like Tris Speaker, Harry Hooper, and Bill Carrigan, all of whom Taylor had a major hand in acquiring. "Taylor never posed as an outstanding judge of baseball talent, but you can't possibly come up with as many fine players and so few duds as he did . . . without keen baseball judgment," Carrigan said.

Nevertheless, the team might have gone farther if not for the excessive meddling of the Boston owner. Before the start of the season, he sent fan favorite and perennial twenty-game winner Cy Young to Cleveland for unproven pitchers Jack Ryan and Charlie Chech and $12,500. According to biographer Reed Browning, Taylor and his management staff believed that Young was "playing on borrowed time and that if he could be exchanged for several promising youngsters before his arm gave out, the gain would be all Boston's."

The opposite turned out to be true, as Ryan and Chech became major league busts. In fact, had Taylor hung on to Young, who went on to notch nineteen wins on the year for the Naps, chances are that Boston would have won the American League pennant in 1909. As it was, the team finished a surmountable nine and a half games behind Detroit.

"You can pick up all the young good ones you want," former batting star Tommy McCarthy presciently told a reporter at the time of the trade, "but the good old ones are very scarce. Cy will win a lot of games for Cleveland. . . . I think it will be Boston's loss for a year or two, for I am not stuck on ball teams that haven't a few old heads."

By this time, the team was operating under a new moniker. Aware that the crosstown Doves, formerly the Beaneaters, had moved away from the red hosiery that had been a distinctive part of their uniforms in 1907, Taylor prudently adopted the color for his own club, which heretofore had been outfitted in a blue design. "From now on we'll wear red stockings and I'm grabbing that name Red Sox," Taylor said. The rechristened Sox would continue to win more games than they lost over the next two seasons but fail to seriously contend for the pennant as a spate of injuries, youthful inexperience, and a lack of overall pitching sealed their fate.

Frustrated by the lack of on-field success and worn down by the incessant pressure associated with the day-to-day running of a major league franchise, Taylor decided to sell his controlling interest in the team to former NL outfielder and Ban Johnson ally James McAleer for $150,000 in 1911.

But before the deal could be consummated, Taylor set into motion plans for the club to abandon the old Huntington Avenue Grounds and to build a glittering new steel and concrete ballpark between Landsdowne and Jersey Streets in Boston's less than fashionable "Fens" area. That structure would become famous as Fenway Park—the "lyric, little bandbox of a ballpark" that novelist John Updike later mythologized in a famous *New Yorker* essay.

Propitiously for Taylor, he retained ownership rights to the park when it was finished and rented it out to McAleer, thus realizing a sizable profit for himself. "Now Taylor could do what he really wanted to, which was to become a landlord," opined the historian Glenn Stout.

In the tumultuous decade ahead, that landlord would witness some of the greatest Boston teams ever assembled exert mastery over an unsuspecting baseball world. The Red Sox dynasty had arrived.

GIANT KILLERS (1912)

Presidential politics dominated the headlines in the spring of 1912. A November general election loomed on the horizon, and former chief executive Theodore Roosevelt was working feverishly to recapture the White House as an "insurgent" Republican. "My hat is in the ring," he declared.

Left unmentioned was how Roosevelt's quixotic candidacy would impact the reelection chances of incumbent William Howard Taft, T. R.'s longtime GOP ally and handpicked successor as commander in chief. Over the previous three years, the two had grown apart politically on a wide range of issues, from tariff reform to conservation. Now they found themselves on opposite ends of an increasingly contentious fight for the Republican nomination.

"I don't understand Roosevelt," Taft confessed to an aide. "I don't know what he is driving at except to make my way more difficult. It is hard, very hard, to see a devoted friendship go to pieces like a rope of sand." But go to pieces it did as Roosevelt became intent on denying Taft a second term.

On the Democratic side, former Princeton University president and New Jersey governor Woodrow Wilson was in the midst of his successful bid for his party's presidential nomination. At heart a progressive reformer, Wilson vowed to rein in what he

CHAPTER TWO

saw as the overweening influence of big business on American society. This goal, he said, could only be accomplished through remedial federal action. "This is the greatest question of all," he insisted, "and to this statesmen must address themselves with an earnest determination to serve the long future and the true liberties of men."

In Lawrence, Massachusetts, striking mill workers scored a major victory over big business when their employers acceded to their demands for higher wages and better working conditions. This "bloodless revolution" was achieved largely through the efforts of William D. "Big Bill" Haywood, the leader of the Industrial Workers of the World. Haywood had offered his services to the strikers shortly after they had walked off their jobs in January. Although he had never been skittish about employing brute force in prior labor–management standoffs, Haywood decided to go the nonviolent route in Lawrence. "When we strike now, we strike with our hands in our pockets," he said. The tactic worked brilliantly, generating popular sympathy for the workers while obliging the mill owners to back down from their earlier intransigent negotiating stance. As the muckraking journalist Lincoln Steffens observed, "Labor has seldom, if ever, won so complete a victory."

Winning was also on the minds of the Red Sox as they gathered for spring training in Hot Springs, Arkansas, in March. Having endured years of mediocre play, this gifted yet maddeningly underachieving squad finally believed it was on the verge of a breakout season. "I don't see how they can stop us from being one of the contenders for the American League championship this year," outfielder Tris Speaker told a reporter. "The boys are pulling together and everyone is anxious for the season to open."

This newfound confidence was due in no small part to an acquisition that new club owner James McAleer had made in mid-January. At his urging, veteran first baseman and former Boston star Garland "Jake" Stahl was brought onboard as player-manager. In terms of attitude, intelligence, and overall leadership ability,

The new Boston field manager and new owner, Jake Stahl and James McAleer, confer with each other before the start of the memorable 1912 season. (Courtesy of the Boston Public Library Print Department, Michael T. McGreevey Collection.)

McAleer could not have made a better choice. Stahl "is the sort of man to inspire the best efforts of those under him," noted one writer. The son of a Civil War veteran who fought on the Union side, Stahl had a happy, if uneventful, upbringing. He was good at athletics and went on to star in football and baseball at the University of Illinois, where he earned a degree in law. In 1903, he signed with Boston and watched from the bench as the team won the first World Series. He was traded to Washington in the off-season and put together several productive seasons for the Senators before finally heading back to Boston in 1908.

Though outwardly reserved, the six-foot, two-inch, 195-pound Stahl commanded the respect of his players through his own hustling brand of play and his take no prisoners managerial approach to the game. "Mr. Stahl will add strength in batting, strength in fielding, and a clever head to the lineup of the Boston team—things the club needed badly [last season]," predicted the venerable *Baseball Magazine*. "With Stahl added, the Red Sox are bound to climb."

Yet it took some doing on McAleer's part to convince Stahl to accept the challenge. A dyed-in-the-wool individualist, Stahl had left baseball abruptly in 1911 to take an executive position with the Woodlawn Trust and Savings Bank in Chicago. He had given no indications of wanting to deviate from this new career path until McAleer approached him in the off-season with a lucrative financial proposition. In return for agreeing to pilot the team, Stahl was tendered a 10 percent ownership stake in the franchise. The offer was simply too good for the lifetime .261 hitter to refuse.

Monetary inducements aside, Stahl could not have been disappointed by the highly talented roster he inherited. With the "Golden Outfield" of George "Duffy" Lewis in left, Tris Speaker in center, and Harry Hooper in right, Boston possessed the finest trio of fly catchers in baseball. "The three of them could field, and they could throw," longtime Boston sportswriter Joe Cashman told author Peter Golenbock in 1992. "You couldn't run on them, couldn't take an extra base. Your life wasn't worth a nickel." Speaker was the main standout.

A Texas native, "Spoke" tore up the Southern League in 1908 with a .350 average. Nor did he disappoint in a Boston uniform a year later. He batted .309 and led the club with a .443 slugging percentage and seven home runs that rookie season. Defensively, he was even better, establishing himself as a preeminent center fielder with a league-leading 319 putouts and thirty-nine assists. "I studied every angle, absorbed every item of information available and practiced constantly until I became a regular," he later said.

As for Lewis and Hooper, they acted as perfect "wing men" to Speaker. A survivor of the San Francisco earthquake of 1906, the stocky five-foot, ten-inch, 170-pound Lewis showed surprising power for someone his size. In 1911, his second year in the majors, he cranked out thirty-two doubles and tied for fourth place in the league in homers with seven. But it was his shotgun arm that garnered the most attention. "If you ever got hit by one of Lewis's throws right in the air, you'd get killed," Cashman contended. "Lewis, in left, never bounced the ball. It was in the air all the way."

Hooper was a converted pitcher who had earned the sobriquet "Ty Cobb of the State League" while playing for Sacramento in the California State League. Not only did he bat a sizzling .344, he also stole thirty-four bases. But these gaudy statistics did not guarantee him a spot on the Boston roster when he arrived for his first big-league spring training camp in 1909. As Hooper recalled, "We'd get the Boston papers and I read that 'this Hooper appears to be a good prospect, but he needs several years of seasoning in the minors before he'll be ready.' That made my blood boil. I *knew* I was good enough to make that team."

He need not have been so concerned. Retained by the team as a fourth outfielder, he hit .282 in eighty-one games. He was elevated to starting status the following season and never looked back. "He comes as near being the perfect outfielder as any man I ever saw," Babe Ruth once commented. "He would take one squint, then turn his back and run to the place where the ball was headed. And in all his career I don't believe he misjudged a half a dozen balls."

While lacking the bona fides of their more celebrated outfield counterparts, the Boston infield was nevertheless solid. Jake Stahl and Larry Gardner exhibited particular skill in holding down the corner positions at first and third respectively. Insofar as Stahl may have been a step slower around the bag due to his year away from the game, he still provided a steady glove. In later comparing Stahl to star New York Giants first baseman Fred Merkle, the veteran baseball scribe Hugh S. Fullerton opined that the former held a "big advantage." Stahl "stretches to meet his throws and helps his infield in many cases," Fullerton wrote. "He saves many a close decision by his ability to reach. Besides, he gets into the path after throws close to the runners better than Merkle does."

Stahl could also hit, leading the league in home runs with ten in 1910 to go with nineteen doubles, sixteen triples, and a .271 average. With regards to Gardner, the University of Vermont product had already made his mark as one of the better all around third basemen in the league, fielding his position flawlessly and batting better than .280 in each of his previous four seasons with the team. "A hell of a ballplayer," teammate Smokey Joe Wood said.

The middle infielders weren't devoid of ability either. Charles Francis "Heinie" Wagner was a dependable presence at shortstop, even though his low-key personality prevented him from gaining much notice outside the clubhouse. A German immigrant's son, Wagner had learned his ball on the makeshift street diamonds of New York City at the turn of the century. He came to Boston in 1906 and, after a brief stint as a backup infielder, earned a starting berth at short the following season. "Quiet and unassuming in his work, he has gradually worked his way to the front rank of all ball players in this country," lauded the *Boston Post* in 1910. Wagner would hit a solid .274 in 1912, in addition to setting career marks in hits (138), RBIs (68), and walks (62).

His double-play partner, twenty-three-year-old second baseman Steve Yerkes, proved handy with the bat as well. After joining the team for the 1911 campaign, the fleet-footed Pennsylvanian got upper management's attention by banging out 140 hits in 142 games. In Yerkes, the *Sporting News* reported, the Sox had "a first rate infielder."

Starting catcher Bill "Rough" Carrigan had a more difficult time establishing himself as a big leaguer. Following a brief cup of coffee with the parent club in 1906, where he batted a forgettable .211 in thirty-seven games, the feisty five-foot, nine-inch, 175-pound backstop from Lewiston, Maine, was sent down to the minors. There he flourished behind the plate, hitting an eye-opening .320 and leading Toronto to the Little World Series championship. Returning to Boston, he took over the regular catching duties and finished eighth in the league in batting with a .296 average in 1909. "I don't think anyone was better at blocking the plate than Bill," extolled third baseman Larry Gardner. "Boy, he was tough."

Tough was not a term many used to describe the Red Sox pitching staff. Outside of twenty-two-year-old fireballer Smokey Joe Wood, who was coming off an impressive twenty-win season in 1911, the rotation was riddled with question marks. Left-hander Ray Collins, who hailed from Colchester, Vermont, had shown flashes of brilliance in his previous three seasons with the team, but he was considered far from a proven commodity due to injury. "His shoulder has not been good this spring, but he thinks it will round into shape as soon as the weather turns warm," noted the Boston sportswriter John J. Hallahan.

Rookies Thomas "Buck" O'Brien and Hugh Bedient looked more promising but had little or no experience against big-league competition. O'Brien, a musically gifted spitball artist from Brockton, Massachusetts, in fact came off as something of a flake. He insisted that his singing on stage in the off-season "kept his arm in shape." "Wonder how," speculated a bemused *Boston Evening Record*.

Rounding out the staff were veterans Charles "Sea Lion" Hall and Eddie Cicotte. Hall, who reportedly received his nickname because of his unique ability to "imitate the bark or call of a sea lion," was a career journeyman whose previous best season had been in

1910 when he went 12–9 with a 1.99 ERA. He had fallen off statistically in 1911 and as a result was not expected to be a big contributor.

Cicotte was a different story. A crafty right-hander who could throw an effective spitter or emery ball, the Springwells, Michigan, native appeared to have all the needed tools to be a successful starter. "He throws with effect practically every kind of ball known to pitching science," marveled the *Sporting News*. But for all his talent, Cicotte had been nothing more than a .500 pitcher for Boston since breaking in with the club in 1908.

When he continued to underachieve in the early part of the 1912 season, a frustrated Sox front office dealt him to the Chicago White Sox for cash. He thrived for a time in the Windy City, registering three twenty-win seasons before gaining everlasting infamy with the 1919 Black Sox for throwing World Series games. "A real tragic case," Larry Gardner said.

Because of these perceived pitching shortcomings, most baseball experts picked the Red Sox to finish a distant third or fourth in the AL behind the two-time defending World Series champion Philadelphia Athletics. The A's, who were managed by the avuncular Connie Mack, fielded a star-studded lineup that featured future Hall of Famers Eddie Collins and Frank "Home Run" Baker. "First and foremost, the statement comes natural that the Philadelphia Athletics have what looks like a sure thing in the American League," the *Sporting News* declared.

Not everyone was in accordance with this opinion, however. "Look out!" interjected Hugh S. Fullerton. "Boston is again on the baseball map. The new regime presents to the long patient Beantown public a ball club which looks second best in the league—and which with a little luck may push the Athletics off their proud perch."

As if to reward Fullerton's faith in them, the Sox did get off to a quick start. They won four of their first five regular season games on the road, including an opening three-game sweep of the New York Highlanders. "The team has been hitting the ball hard, and there have been some fine rallies, while the infielding has been particularly first class," reported the *Boston Globe*. "The presence of Stahl on first base has made a vast difference, and by all accounts Wagner's arm is far better than it was at any time last year. These are only two things, which more than anything else, with the condition of the pitchers of course, the fans expect will make the difference between a fair Red Sox team and really great one."

Howsoever gratifying this road success must have been to the club, it took a decided backseat to the most eagerly anticipated local event of the young baseball season: the official opening of Fenway Park. "The new park . . . will be a notable achievement in baseball architecture," predicted one publication. "It has been needed for some time in Boston, which has always been famed for its baseball enthusiasm and the enormous crowds which support its favorite team."

Built on top of a former swamp in Boston's Fenway district near Kenmore Square, the sprawling new steel and concrete park was part of an explosive wave of newly constructed urban ballparks across the land that were literally transforming the way fans and players experienced the game.

"With a more permanent, sturdier design and ramps to move people quickly up and down the grandstand, the parks were easier for spectators to navigate," write historians Gary Gillette and Eric Enders in their informative 2009 book *Big League Ballparks: The Complete Illustrated History*. "They were also more comfortable for the players, who now had locker rooms at their home parks and when traveling."

Like Forbes Field (Pittsburgh), Comiskey Park (Chicago), League Park (Cleveland), Redland Field (Cincinnati), Shibe Park (Philadelphia), Navin Field (Detroit), the Polo Grounds (New York), and Griffith Stadium (Washington, D.C.), which catered to the large sporting populations of their respective cities, Fenway offered a clean and relatively expansive facility with all the modern amenities, including an electric scoreboard and a convenient adjoining parking lot for fans who opted to drive to the park in their own automobiles.

"The seats were oak, and the red brick façade, done in the Tapestry style, seemed to be almost needlepointed and reminded onlookers of a New England sampler," notes the writer Michael Gershman. Lending further charm to the park were its idiosyncratic dimensions, which extended 321 feet to left, 488 feet to center, and 314 feet to right. And if this weren't quirky enough, a twenty-five-foot wooden fence stood in left field, complete with a ten-foot-high embankment that would soon be dubbed "Duffy's Cliff" in recognition of Duffy Lewis's exceptional defensive skill over the terrain. In later years, the embankment would be removed and the left field wall refashioned with green sheet metal, thus earning the famous nickname of "Green Monster."

It must be noted, however, that these many aesthetic touches and quirks, welcomed though they were, served a broader economic purpose. For the park, as the author George Sullivan points out, had to "conform to the property's peculiar real estate boundaries," which included Lansdowne Street behind the left-field wall and Jersey Street (later renamed Yawkey Way) running parallel to the main grandstand entrance.

That explains why, for example, the third base line extending from home plate had to be positioned "just a little to the left of magnetic north." According to noted baseball chronicler Dan Shaughnessy, "Games in 1912 often started mid-afternoon, and the alignment of Fenway's base paths ensured that the sun would never set in the eyes of the batters. It would be the right fielders who would contend with the sun setting behind the third base line."

Even the construction of "Duffy's Cliff" had a bottom line aspect to it. "The ten-foot embankment in left field was erected not to create excitement during a ballgame, but to make it easier for spectators sitting out there to see the action," wrote journalist and historian Peter Golenbock. "On days when ticket demand was great, the ballpark sat the overflow crowd behind the left fielder. If the area had been flat, the fans in the back rows would not have been able to see over the heads of the fans in front of them."

Related to this, there was a growing awareness in baseball front offices that with the country's booming economic prosperity at the beginning of the twentieth century, the game's traditional business model needed to be adjusted accordingly. Indeed, given the increased competition for the consumer dollar from such popular new leisure-time activities as motion pictures and vaudeville, the sport could no longer afford to limit itself to the urban laboring masses that had flocked to games in the previous century. Frankly, it needed to branch out.

As Gillette and Enders note, "Club owners hoped that these classy new ballparks would lead to a higher-income fan base, and to that end every effort was made to make the parks opulent and luxurious, from designing impressive rotundas to installing the latest technological advances, such as elevators." This, in turn, placed inordinate "pressure" on franchises saddled with aging physical facilities to make upgrades or face rapid declines in attendance. Owners "began to realize that the ballpark itself could be an attraction, even if the team was mediocre," Gillette and Enders write.

Boston had had its share of memorable ballparks over the decades. Perhaps the most noteworthy was the South End Grounds where the Braves, then known as the Beaneaters, had taken up residence in the late nineteenth century. Rebuilt three times since opening for business in 1871, the simple yet elegant all-wooden structure was rectangular in shape and sat astride a local railroad line where present-day Columbus Avenue intersects with Walpole Street.

"With cinders and smoke from passing trains ever present," notes historian Alan E. Foulds, "the site was not highly regarded as prime real estate. Yet because of those tracks and nearby streetcars the field was easily accessible for most Bostonians."

In 1887, the ballpark underwent a major renovation that added a semi-circular upper deck grandstand area complete with six medieval-looking spires and supporting "tulip-shaped columns." Popularly known as the "Grand Pavilion," this boldly unconventional structure seated 6,800 and became an instant magnet for local baseball fans. "What they saw had, from the outside, more in common with the novels of Sir Walter Scott than anything so ignoble [as a simple ballgame]," writes Michael Gershman.

Yet all the public excitement surrounding the revamped ballpark literally went up in smoke less than a decade later. On May 15, 1894, a fire broke out in the right-field bleacher section after a fan carelessly disposed of a cigarette. The flames then spread to the rest of the ballpark, completely enveloping the ornate central grandstand while spilling over to the surrounding neighborhood, causing 177 buildings to be incinerated over a twelve-acre expanse. "At the present time it is impossible to give a complete list of the various families who now find themselves homeless, penniless and in the deepest despair," the *Boston Globe* reported.

Amazingly, the park was rebuilt just a month later but on a vastly cheaper and toned-down scale due to the financial constraints the fire had caused the underinsured team ownership. Gone were the spires and the enticing "Knights of the Round Table" look of the structure. In its place was a more utilitarian, if bland, venue that

In its heyday at the end of the nineteenth century, the South End Grounds represented the grandest baseball venue in the country. (Courtesy of the Boston Public Library Print Department, Sports Temples of Boston Collection.)

would remain standing until 1929, over a decade after the Nationals had decided to abandon its cramped and increasingly decrepit confines for the more spacious Braves Field off Commonwealth Avenue. As Alan E. Foulds writes, the South End Grounds had become "woefully inadequate for a major league team."

Just the opposite was true of the new Fenway Park. Thoroughly modern and state of the art, the ballpark sprang from the determined efforts of John I. Taylor. Looking to reap a sizable financial windfall, the opportunistic Red Sox owner saw the construction of the ballpark as a "can't miss" proposition. That's because he was a stakeholder in the Fenway Realty Company (FRC), a burgeoning business enterprise that his family or more specifically his father, *Boston Globe* owner General Charles H. Taylor, controlled.

The FRC had bought up a sizable chunk of the Fenway district, which until the 1880s had been undesirable swampland. Then Frederick Law Olmstead entered the picture. One of nineteenth-century America's leading landscape architects, Olmstead determined that the area would make an appealing link in his famed Emerald Necklace, an elaborate network of parks that sought to bring such disparate Boston neighborhoods as the Back Bay and South Boston closer together.

"It was a staggering project that not only provided the city with a natural boundary of exceptional beauty," wrote noted Boston historian Thomas H. O'Connor, "but also provided a place where the working people of the city could come with their families to enjoy the beauties of nature." Alas, although the swamp was drained per the direction of Olmstead, enthusiasm for incorporating the Fenway area as parkland eventually faded. In fact, by the turn of the century, "the park idea had died," Michael Gershman writes, "and the Fenway became the last of Boston's neighborhoods to be the product of filled-in land."

The financial stars were thus properly aligned for Taylor. For, as historian Glenn Stout observes, the land "surrounding the Fenway became a real estate speculator's dream—cheap, undeveloped, and an ideal location adjacent to the city's expanding streetcar lines." Taylor and his family immediately grasped the significance, securing much of the available land through the auspices of their holding company, the FRC. "So when he needed a place to build his new ballpark, [Taylor] in effect sold himself an empty plot of land on Jersey Street," notes Stout.

This also helps explain how Taylor's new ballpark acquired its name. As Foulds points out, the branding should be considered "an early form of corporate 'naming rights.'" Indeed, eager to promote the FRC and the local properties it held, Taylor must have felt it was a no-brainer to attach the now familiar Fenway appellation. The irony of this set of circumstances did not escape the later wry notice of Dan Shaughnessy. "If Boston's next baseball facility is named Century 21 Park," he writes, "it would only be consistent with the Taylors' action in 1912."

When it came to the task of actually building the ballpark, Taylor contracted the job out to Osborn Engineering, a Cleveland, Ohio, firm that finished the project on schedule for $650,000. While the price tag may have been steep for the day, Taylor voiced no open concern, which is understandable given his own unique situation. He had already netted a cool $150,000 by selling his controlling stake in the team to new majority owner James McAleer, while still holding deed to the Fenway property. This meant that he would be in the highly enviable and lucrative position of collecting rent from the team as its new landlord. "Sweet deal," Shaughnessy assessed. Additionally, Taylor stood to benefit directly from increased land values which the new park was expected to generate for nearby FRC properties. "There was backslapping all around," Stout maintains.

The backslapping would continue on Opening Day. Originally scheduled for April 18, the Fenway curtain raising had to be delayed two days due to rain. Technically, it was the second curtain raising, as the Sox had played a seven-inning exhibition game against the Harvard University baseball team on April 9. But that game, a 2–0 victory for the host club amid lightly falling spring snowflakes, had been sparsely attended and construction workers had yet to install all the seats or properly prepare the playing field.

April 20 would be different. With the foul weather having finally subsided and the ballpark truly ready for business, most of the twenty-seven thousand in attendance came away favorably impressed. And why wouldn't they be? The park represented the biggest venue for athletic competition in the city's long and proud history, with the capacity to hold thirty-five thousand fans.

Too bad then that most of the hoopla surrounding the park's launching was superseded by news that the luxury liner *Titanic* had sunk in the North Atlantic following a collision with an iceberg. More than fifteen hundred people lost their lives in what remains one of the greatest sea disasters of all time. "A superstitious sort might have interpreted this juxtaposition of events as a bad omen," posits Dan Shaughnessy.

Be that as it may, Boston mayor John "Honey Fitz" Fitzgerald did get to throw out the ceremonial first pitch. That the maternal grandfather of President John F. Kennedy received this unique honor was only appropriate. A longtime baseball enthusiast, the charismatic and independent-minded Fitzgerald delighted in going to games and mingling with his fellow fans, most of whom he was not shy about sharing a boisterously good time with. In 1904, he had even come tantalizingly close to purchasing the team, but the deal collapsed at the last minute due to the opposition of AL president Ban Johnson. "Johnson would countenance only owners he could control, and Honey Fitz did not fit into that category," concluded writer Roger I. Abrams.

Still, whatever residual disappointment he might have harbored with regard to this failed transaction was nowhere to be found on this particular festive occasion. "The day was ideal," confirmed writer T. H. Murnane. "The bright sun brought out the bright colors of the flags and bunting that decorated the big grandstand and gave the new uniforms of the players a natty look."

Speaking of the uniforms, the Red Sox entered the 1912 campaign in especially attractive threads. In comparison to previous seasons,

Fenway Park drew mostly rave reviews when it first opened in 1912. "The mammoth plant, with its commodious fittings, met with distinct approval," observed one newspaper. (Courtesy of the Library of Congress.)

Smokey Joe Wood had a regular season for the ages in 1912, winning 34 games to go with 10 shutouts and 258 strikeouts. "My friend, there isn't a man alive who throws harder than Smokey Joe Wood," Walter Johnson said. (Courtesy of the Library of Congress.)

when the players were forced to wear such gaudy all-wool wear as a lace-collared shirt with a cartoonish big red sock in the middle, the new ensemble was buttoned-down and appealing.

In fact, there were two different sets of home and away uniforms with matching caps, foreseeing a trend modern ball clubs, including the Red Sox, would adopt as standard operating procedure in the twenty-first century. The Boston home jerseys, for example, consisted of either a crisp all-white front with striking red lettering spelling out the team's name or a tasteful pinstripe version that was devoid of any script. Either way, both uniforms had the tendency to stand out, which no doubt pleased players and fans alike.

As for the contest itself, it was a taut affair which saw the Sox defeat the Highlanders 7–6 in extra innings. Tris Speaker provided the game-winning hit, a two-out bullet in the bottom of the eleventh that whistled through the left side of the New York infield and scored teammate Steve Yerkes from third.

Wrote Paul Shannon, "Three hours before, a curious, impatient crowd had gathered within the big enclosure, hoping for a Red Sox victory and a fourth straight win from New York. It was well toward twilight when that same crowd, no longer a mildly enthusiastic body but a yelling, cheering mob, hurried back to the four corners of Greater Boston to spread the news of an uphill fight, a thrilling finish and a great 11th inning defeat for [the] Highlanders."

The dramatic victory served as an augury for things to come. Building upon their strong head start, the Sox did the baseball equivalent of lapping the field. By the beginning of July, they were 52–24 with a double-digit lead over their main rivals, the heavily favored Athletics. Helping make the team's runaway success possible was Tris Speaker.

At age twenty-four, "the bounding cowboy of the Texas plains" was entering his prime as a Hall of Fame outfielder. "Speaker played a real shallow center field," remembered his longtime friend and roommate Smokey Joe Wood, "and he had that terrific instinct—at the crack of the bat he'd be off with his back to the infield, and then he'd turn and glance over his shoulder at the last minute and catch the ball so easy it looked like nothing to it, nothing at all. Nobody else was even in the same *league* with him."

Yet it was Speaker's bat that spoke the loudest in 1912 as he hit a lofty .383 with fifty-three doubles, ten homers, and ninety runs knocked in. He also stole fifty-two bases, a club record that stood until outfielder Tommy Harper broke it in 1973 with fifty-four thefts. "I always could hit," Speaker later said. "Really, I couldn't tell you how I hit. I just hit 'em. That's all I know."

In recognition of his stellar contributions on the field, Speaker was named the AL recipient of the Chalmers Award, a prestigious annual baseball honor that anticipated the Most Valuable Player Award of later years. It went to the individual who proved himself to be "the most important and useful player to his club and to the league at large in point of deportment and value of services rendered."

Another leading factor in Boston's rise to preeminence was the surprising quality of its starting pitching staff. Wood, Hugh Bedient, Buck O'Brien, Ray Collins, and Sea Lion Hall all finished the year with thirteen wins or better, a fact that no self-respecting baseball prognosticator could have predicted, given the uncertainty surrounding the rotation that spring. As E. D. Soden of *Baseball Magazine* wrote, "Boston has had a good club for some years, but its principal misfortunes seemed to hover in the pitcher's box. Now, however . . . there is no such difficulty."

Smokey Joe Wood set the standard. So dominating was his performance on the mound that when all-time strikeout king Walter Johnson of the Washington Senators was asked if he threw harder than Wood, he answered, "My friend, there isn't a man alive who throws harder than Smokey Joe Wood."

Allowing just a shade under two runs a game, Wood reeled off sixteen consecutive victories from July 8 to September 15, including a dazzling 1–0 decision over Johnson at Fenway on September 6. "Clark Griffith [Washington owner] had come to town early, and he had challenged me and the Boston management," Wood recalled later. "It was like a big prize fight. The papers printed the heights and weights of Johnson and myself, and dimensions of our biceps and our triceps."

Not surprisingly, fan interest grew to a fever pitch as a raucous, overflow crowd of over thirty-two thousand crammed into the ballpark to witness "the most stirring pitching duel in the history of the American League." "I never saw so many people in my life," Wood said. "In fact the fans were put on the field an hour before the game started, and it was so crowded down there I hardly had room to warm up."

Despite the claustrophobic conditions, Wood permitted just six hits over nine innings to go with nine strikeouts and three walks. "Joe, back there, had a fast ball which was as effective and baffling as Walter's, if not just as speedy and blinding," recalled Bill Carrigan. "And Joe had a much better curve. His hook exploded. Johnson's No. 2 was just a wrinkle. He just didn't need it with his speed."

Johnson was equally impressive, fanning five and giving up five hits. However, one of those hits was a two-out double by Tris Speaker down the third base line in the sixth inning. Speaker then scored on a Duffy Lewis "flair" that fell just beyond the outstretched reach of diving Washington outfielder Dan Moeller in right. Ever the gentleman, Johnson tried to comfort a disconsolate Moeller afterward. "Don't feel badly," he told his teammate. "I should have struck him out."

Although he had emerged from this epic showdown a winner, Wood never let it go to his head. "I can't really say that I beat Walter," he explained. "He was the greatest pitcher that ever lived. But, he didn't have a club behind him, and I had a good one."

The story of Wood's rise to pitching stardom is one of initiative, pluck, and an unswerving belief in his own extraordinary abilities. Born on October 25, 1889, in Kansas City, Missouri, Wood spent most of his early childhood in the Midwest. His father, John Wood, was a University of Pennsylvania graduate who had built up a successful legal practice in Chicago. He married the former Rebecca Stevens and appeared destined to live out his days in relative bourgeois comfort.

However, after a decade of being a lawyer in the Windy City, John grew restless. He "got the gold fever and joined the Alaskan gold rush,"

Wood later told author Donald Honig. "He spent some time there trying to make his fortune, same as a lot of other people. No, he didn't strike it rich. As a matter of fact he was lucky to get out alive. The Yukon River was frozen over, you see." Wrapping his legs in gunnysacks, the elder Wood managed to walk out of the then largely untamed U.S. territory, averaging thirty miles a day.

But this Alaskan adventure had exacted a steep physical toll. "When he got out the doctors told him the only way he'd get the circulation and the feeling back in his legs was to go barefoot in the sand," Wood remembered. "So he went down to the gold strike in California and Nevada. The climate might have been better down there, but his luck stayed the same."

Returning to Chicago, John got antsy again and decided to move his young family to several different western locales before finally settling down in Ness City, Kansas, in 1905. The family's chief mode of transportation was a covered wagon. "They talk about this being an on-the-go society today, what with the automobile and super highways and all that, but it seems to me that Americans were always a restless people," Wood said. "Back then those wagon wheels were always grinding, and wherever you went you met people going in the opposite direction."

In spite of the constant uprooting, young Joe managed to find the time to pursue what was already becoming a consuming passion in his life: baseball. "I always wanted to be a pitcher and used to throw everything from snowballs to rocks trying to get my arm in shape so that I could shoot the ball over the plate," he later revealed. "I threw whenever I got the chance and when I was seventeen years old I was pitching on a fairly good country team."

His pitching became so impressive that he attracted the attention of a barnstorming Bloomer Girls group. A loose collection of professional women's teams that played "up and down the country" starting in the 1880s, the Bloomer Girls were not above employing a few "ringers" of the opposite sex, provided they were willing to put on a dress and artfully disguise their gender. "There were four guys on the team," Wood said. "The other five were girls. We dressed in hotel rooms. The other guys had to wear wigs, but I had a baby face, and didn't need one."

In 1907 Wood signed with the Cedar Rapids Rabbits of the local Three-I League for the less than munificent sum of $90 a month. Before he even played an inning, however, he was sent packing by club owner Belden Hill to the Hutchinson club of the Western Association. "He didn't sell me, he just *gave* me away," Wood fumed.

Unfazed, the skinny right-hander put up big numbers with Hutchinson: twenty wins and two hundred strikeouts. Already, his blazing arm speed was making an impression on fans and players alike. "That boy is one of the most wonderful pitchers I ever saw," raved veteran Cleveland pitcher Addie Joss. "He makes my fastball

The grandfather of President John F. Kennedy, Boston mayor John "Honey Fitz" Fitzgerald enjoyed nothing better than throwing out the first pitch of a new season, whether it was at the old Huntington Avenue Grounds pictured here or at the new Fenway Park. (Courtesy of the Boston Public Library Print Department, Sports Temples of Boston Collection.)

look like a floater." The Kansas City Blues of the American Association purchased his contract for the following season, but Wood faltered, compiling a 7–12 mark in twenty-four appearances. Still, he showed enough stuff to turn the heads of most big-league scouts. "Word got around, I guess, that I was a good pitcher," he said.

Among the interested suitors were the Red Sox, who inked the eighteen-year-old phenom to a contract late in the 1908 season. "Cy Young was on that Red Sox team," Wood recalled. "He was around forty years old at that time, but I don't think you could say he was over the hill since he pitched 300 innings that year and won twenty-one games. No, he didn't pay much attention to me. I don't think we talked to one another at all. I was just an unknown kid coming onto the club."

He would not remain unknown for long. After compiling a mediocre 24–21 record in his first two plus seasons with Boston, Wood broke out with an outstanding 23–17 campaign in 1911. He registered 226 strikeouts and a stingy 2.02 ERA in 276 innings of work. He also tossed a no-hitter against the St. Louis Browns at the Huntington Grounds on July 29. Wood was "invincible from bell to bell," reported R. E. McMillin of the *Boston Herald*. "Three opponents reached first against him. Two of these were given passes. One, Happy Hogan, got in the way of a slow ball and was punched in the ribs. Twelve strikeouts fell to his share, the three men at the top of the visiting list whiffing no less than eight times."

Enabling this success was a fiery, competitive attitude that many found off-putting. "He talked out of the corner of his mouth and used language that would have made a steeple horse jockey blush," remembered Hugh S. Fullerton. "He challenged all opponents and dilated upon their pedigrees." Nor did he hurt his cause with his bat or glove.

A career .283 hitter, Wood had surprising power for someone who barely tipped the scales at 150 pounds. In 1912, he punched out thirteen doubles, a triple, and a homer in 124 at-bats. He would later ply his impressive offensive skills as an outfielder for the Cleveland Indians, batting in as many as ninety-two runs in 1922. "Doggone, I was a *ballplayer*, not just a pitcher," he said.

As for his defense, Wood was ranked among the finest fielding pitchers in all of baseball. "When 'Woody' was on the mound there was an extra infielder in the game," praised former teammate Marty McHale. "Not only was he a great bunt 'hawk' but he invariably knocked down any hard hit ball that came close to the pitcher's box." Wood also made a special point of providing backup to his fellow infielders, especially at first and third. Recalled McHale, "It was a great source of delight for him to retrieve an 'overthrow' and then cut down the astounded base runner at the next base with a lightning like throw which arrived just an instant before said runner entered an extra base in his book."

Nevertheless, Wood was under no delusion as to what made him special. "Nobody was faster than me," he later maintained. Indeed, as word of his remarkable pitching deeds grew, Boston writers fell over themselves trying to come up with an appropriate moniker to hang on the young hurler. Initially, the "Kansas Cyclone" was embraced until Paul Shannon of the *Boston Post* saw him warming up one day. "This kid certainly throws smoke," he exclaimed. The description struck an immediate popular chord.

With "Smokey Joe" leading the way, the Red Sox easily wrapped up the AL pennant with a record 104 victories. But awaiting them in the World Series were the New York Giants, winners of two straight NL crowns. Managed by the cantankerous John McGraw, who once declared that there was "but one game and that game is baseball," the Giants were considered the prohibitive favorites going into the best-of-seven championship series.

The team boasted a powerful hitting attack, sparked by five-time .300 hitter and league MVP Lawrence Joseph "Laughing Larry" Doyle. An emotionally high-strung second baseman who scored an average of eighty-eight runs per season, Doyle possessed as much pop in his fists as he did in his bat. He once decked a fan in a Cincinnati hotel lobby for simply rubbing him the wrong way.

He is also credited with uttering the famous line "It's great to be young and a Giant," after leading the senior circuit with twenty-five triples in 1911.

First baseman Fred Merkle complemented Doyle's steady bat with a team-leading eleven homers and eighty-four RBIs. Long remembered for his "bonehead" baserunning error that cost the Giants the 1908 pennant during a crucial late-season game against the Chicago Cubs, Merkle was an accomplished line-drive hitter who played in six World Series during his sixteen-year big-league career.

On the mound, the Giants were paced by ace extraordinaire Christy Mathewson. "He could throw a ball into a tin cup at pitching range," one amazed contemporary observed. Using such pinpoint control along with a screwball that consistently baffled hitters, Mathewson won twenty games or better an astonishing twelve consecutive times from 1903 to 1914. His pitching gifts aside, the boyishly handsome "Matty" also came to be seen as a potent symbol for his age: a flesh-and-blood Frank Merriwell character who put fair play and his devotion to Christian piety above all else.

Whether this romanticized image was accurate or not was immaterial. Millions of fans across the country believed it, due to the near rapturous media coverage he received during this era. "Christy Mathewson brought something to baseball no one else had ever given the game," the esteemed sports chronicler Grantland Rice said of the Bucknell-educated pitcher. "He handed the game a touch of class, an indefinable lift in culture."

For certain, Mathewson's very appearance at a ballgame could electrify an audience. "I can still see Christy Mathewson making his lordly entrance," longtime pitching rival Mordecai "Three Finger" Brown later related. "He'd always wait until about ten minutes before game time, then he'd come from the clubhouse across the field in a long linen duster like auto drivers wore in those days, and at every step the crowd would yell louder and louder."

Off the field, Mathewson affected an entirely different manner. He was private to the point of being reclusive, avoiding contact with

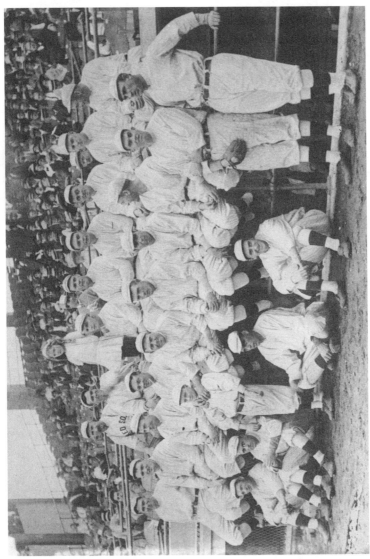

The American League Champion Red Sox would win a record 104 victories in 1912 and go on to meet the highly touted New York Giants in the World Series. (Courtesy of the Library of Congress.)

his adoring public whenever possible. "I owe everything I have to the fans when I'm out there on the mound," he once explained, "but I owe the fans nothing and they owe me nothing when I'm not pitching."

Such reticence never proved a problem for John McGraw. Combative, loud, profane, and uncompromising, the "Little Napoleon" made a special point of letting his players know who was boss. "With my team I am an 'absolute czar,'" he once said. "My men know it. I order plays and they obey. If they don't, I fine them."

Not everyone bought into his authoritarian regime. "You couldn't seem to do anything right for him, ever," complained one former player. "If something went wrong it was always your fault, not his. . . . He was always so grouchy." Still, there is no denying McGraw's demonstrated success on the baseball diamond. In his thirty seasons at the helm of the Giants, he finished either first or second twenty-one times to go along with three World Series championships. "The game of ball is only fun for me when I'm in front and winning," he freely admitted. "I don't care a bag of peanuts for the rest of the game."

The World Series opened on October 8 before a mostly partisan audience of thirty-six thousand at New York's Polo Grounds, a horseshoe-shaped concrete and steel edifice which sat astride the Harlem River under the imposing shadow of Coogan's Bluff. Although greatly outnumbered, a full contingent of Royal Rooters, that fanatical band of Sox enthusiasts who had gained national prominence during the 1903 World Series, made the trek down from Boston to cheer on their Hose. "They made lots of noise and kept it up," reported the *New York Times*. "Long before the game began they were singing the old ditty 'Tessie,' which was popular way back during the 1903 Series. The Red Sox rooters knew it as a lucky song, so even if it was old they still warbled it."

Smokey Joe Wood received the starting nod for Boston and did not disappoint, striking out eleven and walking just two in a complete game, 4–3 victory over the Giants. "I was throwing hard that day, very hard," Wood later reminisced. Despite this fact, the host

New Yorkers did not go down easily. They jumped out to a 2–0 lead in the bottom of the third inning, compliments of a two-run single up the middle by Red Murray.

But spitballing Giant rookie Jeff Tesreau, a surprise pitching choice by McGraw, couldn't hold the lead, giving up a run in the sixth and three more in the seventh. "Harry Hooper got a big hit in that inning and Steve Yerkes knocked in two runs with a hit," said Wood, who proceeded to set down the Giants in order over the next two innings.

The bottom of the ninth was a different story. The Boston ace got roughed up for a run and put the potential tying and winning tallies on second and third with only one out. "Wood had grown white around the gills . . . and he was showing signs of his desperate resolve," wrote Hugh S. Fullerton. Wood nevertheless hung tough, punching out the next two New York batters, Art Fletcher and Doc Crandall, on straight fastballs to end the contest. "Well, I threw so hard I thought my arm would fly right off my body," Wood said.

Game 2 offered more nail-biting excitement, albeit without a clear-cut resolution. The Sox and Giants fought to a 6–6 tie over eleven innings at Fenway in a sloppy contest that had to be called due to darkness. "A couple of longshoremen togged out in ring scenery would have given about as clever an exhibition of the fine art of boxing as some of the contenders did of the technique of the national pastime," opined the *Boston Herald*.

Altogether the teams committed six errors, including a whopping five on the Giants side. Still, there was plenty to cheer about for the thirty thousand Boston fans who braved the unseasonably cold temperatures to attend the game. The Sox offense was in top form, racking up ten base hits and seventeen total bases against Christy Mathewson. "I think today's game, while it did not end in a victory, shows that we can hit the New York twirler, whose work today must have tired him out," remarked Boston skipper Jake Stahl.

Indeed, Mathewson at times appeared overmatched, especially against Tris Speaker. The Big Texan collected two extra base hits

In the lion's den: The Red Sox at New York's famed Polo Grounds for game 1 of the 1912 World Series against John McGraw's Giants. (Courtesy of the Library of Congress.)

and scored the game-tying run in the bottom of the tenth when his triple to center was misplayed into an unofficial inside-the-park home run by the Giants defense.

Wrote Frank Sibley of the *Globe*, "Around the base lines Speaker tore with the air thrilling to the excited shout that never ceased. He was past first before the ball was retrieved, past second when it was thrown. He would make third—he made third—he was checked—he stumbled—and charged up the final base-line to the plate. Up came the ball, Speaker plunged, slid across the plate in a smother of dust. In a flash, two men were clawing the ground desperately—[Giants catcher Art Wilson] grabbing at the ball, Tris crawling back to the home plate, which he had over-slid. But he was safe—and the game was saved."

Boston's batting attack had been superb; its pitching proved otherwise. Sox starter Ray Collins surrendered an early 3–0 lead and got shelled for nine hits and five earned runs in seven and one-third innings.

"It was not Collins' day, the weather being far too cool for the big Vermont southpaw, who stiffens up very quickly when the air is at all chilly," wrote the great Walter Johnson, who was covering the Series as a special assignment columnist. "Collins is one of those pitchers who must keep his arm moving all the time when he is working in anything but warm weather, and it was very noticeable . . . that whenever the game was delayed for a short time Collins was stiff."

Having had victory snatched away by their not so gracious hosts the day before, the Giants regained their footing in game 3 with a 2–1 triumph that evened the Series at a game apiece. Outfielder Josh Devore took home the hero honors for New York. His catch off a smash to right center by Sox backup catcher Forrest "Hick" Cady with two out and the winning run aboard in the bottom of the ninth inning sealed the victory for the Giants.

"Devore was tearing down the field, and while under a full head of steam he leaped into the air, and with hands extended over his head and his back to the infield, he came out of the air with the ball," wrote the *Boston Globe*'s T. H. Murnane. Unfortunately, not many in attendance saw the game-saving catch. A thick fog had settled over Fenway, encouraging the popular belief that Cady's drive had cleared the bases and won the game for the Sox. "Only when [the fans] read in the next day's papers that Devore caught the ball—[umpire Silk] O'Loughlin making the call—did they realize that Boston hadn't won the game," noted author Ray Robinson.

From the perspective of the Red Sox dugout, however, there was never any doubt as to the legitimacy of Devore's grab. "He made the catch while in a very awkward position, but he made it, and that is what saved the game for the Giants," Tris Speaker maintained.

Lost in all the postgame controversy was the brilliant pitching performance of Rube Marquard. The Sox could muster only seven hits and a walk against the stylish Giant left-hander, who spent his off-seasons touring the vaudeville circuit as a performer. "Marquard never had better control in his life, especially of his curveball, and he mixed this one up with his fast one so that the Boston batters did not have a chance," lauded teammate Christy Mathewson.

The Series shifted back to New York for game 4 and once again Smokey Joe Wood was sensational. He went the full nine innings, scattering nine hits and fanning eight in a 3–1 win. Wood even stood out at the plate, going two for four and batting in a run. "JOE THE GIANT KILLER," proclaimed the *Boston Globe* in a front-page cartoon by Wallace Goldsmith, which depicted a pint-sized Wood resting his weary body on a pile of slain behemoths. "WHEW! SOME JOB," offers the Wood caricature.

"Wood pitched beautiful ball," conceded Larry Doyle. "He was never in the hole, always had the situation in hand. He used his curve more today than he did [in game 1] and kept breaking it over the outside corner of the plate. He showed fine headwork in his pitching, for he knew that we expected nothing but speed and that we had prepared for it."

Larry Gardner contributed to the victory with two run-producing hits, including a leadoff triple in the second inning that he was subsequently able to score on following a passed ball. "Gardner got me in the hole . . . and I had to lay the ball over the plate too good for him," lamented Giant starter Jeff Tesreau afterward. "He appreciated it, for he drove to right field for three bases."

Hugh Bedient picked up seamlessly where Wood left off in game 5 as he outdueled Christy Mathewson in a 2–1 victory at Fenway. Bedient, one earned run on three hits, kept the Giants at bay with a steady diet of fastballs. "He was in no very serious holes and there were very few balls hit hard off him, and the team had but few hard chances," noted Walter Johnson approvingly. "Bedient had something on every ball he pitched, and he knew what he was doing with every ball he threw up there, pitching a very heady, cool game from start to finish."

Even John McGraw, who normally parceled out compliments to the opposition about as often as Haley's Comet made an appearance, couldn't help but tip his cap to the tall Boston right-hander. "I must give this young pitcher credit for twirling a great game," the Giants field general commented. "He had practically no curve ball, but he did not need one . . . his high, fast ball was one that my men could do nothing with."

Harry Hooper and Steve Yerkes provided the needed spark offensively for the Sox as their back-to-back triples in the bottom of the third keyed a two-run surge that put the contest away.

Finding themselves in the envious position of being up three games to one and a mere victory away from the championship, the Red Sox to a man looked forward to closing things out at the Polo Grounds the next day. Their optimism seemed well justified. Up to this point, the Giants had collectively failed to live up to their press clippings and the Sox had their ace, a still strong Smokey Joe Wood, ready to take the mound on short rest.

James McAleer had other ideas, however. The Boston owner approached Stahl the night before the anticipated clincher and informed his player-manager that instead of Wood, he wanted O'Brien to start. "We're ahead . . . and can afford to take chances," he explained.

McAleer's request was not unreasonable. O'Brien had pitched effectively in the third game, and the team would still have Wood available with an extra day's rest if a game 7 proved necessary. It also must not have escaped McAleer's keen entrepreneurial mind, as historian Glenn Stout writes, that an O'Brien loss would ensure at least one more game back in Boston, where a large gate and "another lucrative Fenway payday" was expected. Either way, he couldn't lose.

Ever the good soldier, Stahl bowed to his superior's wishes. It was a decision he would soon come to regret as O'Brien couldn't get beyond the first inning the next day, coughing up five runs on a balk and six hits. "It was only too plain to the boys sitting behind the plate that the Boston moist-ball artist had 'nothing,' in the language of the ball field," opined the *Globe*.

Ray Collins came out of the bullpen and pitched shutout ball the rest of the way, but it was too little, too late. The Giants won 5–2, forcing the series back to Boston. In defeat, Stahl did his best to shrug off his obvious disappointment. O'Brien "didn't get the 'breaks' and we will have to try to end the series [at Fenway]," he commented. His players were in a far less forgiving mood. They openly complained of O'Brien's lackluster performance during the long train ride home, and Paul Wood, Smokey Joe's brother, engaged in fisticuffs with the sensitive right-hander after having lost a sizable wager on the contest. "For Christ's sake, I did the best I could!" O'Brien exclaimed.

Game 7 brought only more grief. Smokey Joe started his third Series game for Boston and, like O'Brien the previous day, got clobbered, allowing six runs on seven hits in just one inning of work. Nor were the visiting New Yorkers content to stop there. They added five more runs against an ineffectual Sea Lion Hall in relief to secure a Series-tying 11–4 victory.

"Wood could not have gotten by in a bush league on a dark day with the stuff he [threw]," needled a clearly gloating Larry Doyle afterward. "He did not have anything on the ball, and when he tried to send up his fast one, you could count the stitches on the seams."

R. E. McMillin of the *Boston Herald* concurred. "It was a Smokeless Joe that stepped out into the teeth of the tempest yesterday," he wrote. "He ambled into the middle of the pasture and then all of a sudden found himself beset on all sides by the Gargantuans. His little sling, once so effective, refused to work. The Giants simply crowded up with their cudgels untethered and smashed the first thing that came anywhere near the platter."

Wood's weak performance was not the only hot topic of conversation emerging from the contest. Just prior to the first pitch, a riot almost broke out in the ballpark when the Royal Rooters discovered that their regular seats in the left-field bleachers section had been inexplicably assigned to other paying customers by Sox management.

"Despite their protests," noted a sympathetic reporter, "the rooters who have loyally followed Boston's baseball fortune all through the season, who have warmed the bleacher seats through wind and weather, who have accompanied the Sox into the hostile land of the Giants, and yelled themselves hoarse were turned away [by mounted police] and forced to scramble hither and dither for scant standing room from which only occasional peeps of the players could be obtained."

The fracas left enough of a sour impression with the Rooters that they boycotted the eighth and deciding game the following afternoon. They were scarcely missed, for the Sox and the Giants engaged in an epic baseball battle, one that writer Frederick G. Lieb described as running "the entire gamut of human emotions."

It began inauspiciously enough. Starters Hugh Bedient and Christy Mathewson exchanged goose eggs on the scoreboard until the top of the third inning, when New York's Red Murray drove in Josh Devore with a line-drive double to left center that Tris Speaker uncharacteristically muffed. "Speaker all but clutched the ball, just barely reaching it with his finger tips," reported the *Herald*.

The Giants threatened to add to that 1–0 advantage in the fifth, but Harry Hooper made the defensive play of the game, if not the Series. As Joe Wood recounted, "Larry Doyle hit a terrific drive to deep right center, and Harry ran back at full speed and *dove* over the railing, and into the crowd and in some way, I'll never figure out quite how, he caught the ball—I think with his bare hand. It was almost impossible to believe even when you saw it."

Sox bats remained silent until the home half of the seventh. Stahl reached second on a one-out "Texas Leaguer" to short left center that fell through for a hit. He advanced to third on a Hick Cady flyout before reserve outfielder Olaf Henriksen was tapped to hit for Bedient, who left the game with a final pitching line of one earned run on seven hits.

Henriksen, popularly known as "Swede" in honor of his Nordic heritage, was considered among the finest pinch hitters in the league. "He was one of those rare fellows who could go up cold and hit any sort of pitching," Tris Speaker later said. On this occasion, he was more than up to the challenge, doubling in Stahl for the tying score. But any chance at further heroics was erased when next batter Harry Hooper flied out.

With the score now knotted at one all, Wood was brought in from the bullpen to pitch the eighth. "I don't know if I had any butterflies . . . but let's say I was *impressed* by the situation," Wood later confessed. "Not only is it the last game of the World Series and it's all tied up, but there's Christy Mathewson out there on the other side, and pitching just beautifully."

In point of fact, Wood was none too shabby himself, giving up no runs in the eighth and ninth. But he ran into some difficulty in the tenth. Red Murray hit a one-out double that bounced into the left-field stands. Fred Merkle followed up with a single that drove in Murray for New York's go ahead run. Although Wood retired the next two hitters to get out of the frame, the proverbial genie had been let out of the bottle.

Down to their final at-bat and facing baseball's reigning "Knight in Shining Armor" on the mound, the Sox looked like sure goners as they entered the bottom of the tenth. Leading off for Boston was pinch hitter Clyde Engle, a .234 hitting part-time infielder who

Outfielder Fred Snodgrass would forever be known as the man who cost the Giants the 1912 championship when he dropped a crucial and easily catchable fly ball during the bottom of the tenth inning in game 8. (Courtesy of the Library of Congress.)

appeared in only fifty-seven games on the year. After falling into a quick 0–2 hole against Mathewson, Engle lifted a routine fly ball to Giant outfielder Fred Snodgrass in center.

What happened next was one of the most unlikely episodes in all of World Series history. Snodgrass, a standout outfielder who played nine years in the majors, dropped the ball. "It was so high that Engle was sitting on second base before I could get it back to the infield," Snodgrass later explained.

As embarrassing as the error was, Snodgrass kept his composure. This was no time to panic. When next batter Harry Hooper smashed a line drive over his head in deep left center, he expertly hauled it down on a dead sprint, robbing the Sox right-fielder of an extra base hit.

But Mathewson was not out of the woods yet. Needing just two outs to close out the game and earn the Giants their first World Series championship since 1905, he issued a base on balls to Steve Yerkes on four straight pitches. This set up a situation with runners on first and second and the ever dangerous Speaker coming to bat.

Hunkering down, Mathewson induced Speaker to hit a weak pop-up toward first on a fadeaway. However, Giant first baseman Fred Merkle was slow to react and he yelled for catcher John "Chief" Meyers to make the play. "Meyers chased the ball but it was going away from him and finally Merkle charged but he was too late and couldn't hold the ball," Speaker recalled.

Given this unexpected reprieve, "Spoke" confidently informed Mathewson that the miscue would cost him the game. As if to demonstrate he was a man of his word, Speaker lashed Mathewson's next pitch to right field for a hit, scoring Engle to tie the game. "I didn't miss the second chance," he said.

With the proverbial roof now caving in on the Giants, Mathewson intentionally walked Duffy Lewis to load the bases and set up a potential inning-ending double play. But Larry Gardner foiled the strategy by driving a sacrifice fly to deep right that allowed Yerkes to scamper in with the game and Series winner. "I just wanted to get it to the outfield," Gardner said.

The Sox victory set off a riotous celebration within the ballpark that quickly spread to the entire city. Observed T. H. Murnane of the *Boston Globe*, "Words were never invented that could fully describe the outburst of insane enthusiasm that went thundering around Fenway yesterday afternoon as Steve Yerkes crossed the rubber with the winning run in the 10th inning. Men hugged each other, women became hysterical, youths threw their caps in the air, one man in the bleachers fell in a dead faint, strong hearts lost a beat and started off again at double time."

Truth be told, Boston was in dire need of some good news. Since being founded by John Winthrop and his hearty band of Puritan followers back in 1630 as the original "City on the Hill," the Massachusetts Bay port town had boasted the distinction of being the "Hub of the Universe," a vital commercial, cultural, and intellectual center in the New World. Whether it was leading the fight against British colonial rule in the 1770s or championing the cause of the abolition of slavery before the Civil War or becoming a major manufacturing mecca during the early years of the Industrial Revolution, Boston had always been in the forefront of social change and technological and economic innovation. "Boston was one of the most American of cities," argued the writer Martin Green. "It was a community that tried to embody an idea." And that idea revolved around the notion of progress. Confident of its institutions and its flinty Yankee values of hard work and perseverance, the city never faltered in its belief that it was a latter day "Athens of America."

But by the dawn of the twentieth century, Boston's once lofty self-regard had plunged into new depths of despair as a combination of economic decline, political corruption, poor civic leadership, and changing cultural values left it a decaying monument to a distant and now bygone era. James Michael Curley was now the face of the city, not Oliver Wendell Holmes.

"We are vanishing into provincial obscurity," griped one prominent citizen. "America has swept from our grasp. The future is beyond us." And replacing Boston as the country's enlightened new epicenter was New York City, the Sparta to Beantown's Athens in the jaundiced eyes of its Back Bay and Beacon Hill Brahmin inhabitants. Thus defeating a team representing the "Empire City," the city that had usurped Boston's "rightful" place in the nation's collective consciousness, was no small feat.

Amidst all the shouting and tumult following the game, no Giant took the loss harder than Snodgrass. He achieved official goat status for his "$30,000 Muff," the amount of money he and his teammates were denied by failing to secure a winner's share of the Series gate receipts. "Write in the pages of World's Series history the name of Snodgrass," editorialized an unsympathetic *New York*

Times. "Write it large and black. Not as a hero; truly not. Put him rather with Merkle, who was in such a hurry that he gave away a National League championship. Snodgrass was in such a hurry that he gave away a world championship."

For his part, a clearly disappointed Mathewson went out of his way to defend his now much maligned teammate. "You can't blame a player for a physical error," he said. "That poor fellow feels miserable enough."

None of this mattered to jubilant Boston fans, of course. Basking in the triumphant afterglow of "the most desperately contested World Series on record," they feted their team at a raucous downtown victory parade on October 17, which featured a beaming Honey Fitz leading a procession of automobiles carrying "the Champions of the World" from Fenway to Faneuil Hall.

"This demonstration is the greatest that I have ever witnessed in Faneuil Hall," the Boston mayor proclaimed during a rally at the end of the motorcade. "It shows what Boston people think of those who fight for Boston and win. Your fame is not Boston's alone, because wherever the baseball sport is recognized, and that means every part of the United States because baseball is a national game, you are heroes."

Also enthusiastically taking part in the festivities were the Royal Rooters, who had gotten over their earlier contretemps with Sox management when team owner James McAleer issued a public apology. "We regret very much that this unfortunate affair should have occurred to mar what was in every respect the most sensational series of games ever played," McAleer had stated, "and we appreciate the splendid support and encouragement given the Red Sox in their efforts to bring to Boston the baseball championship of the world."

This high-profile mea culpa notwithstanding, no one came away from the Boston victory with a greater sense of satisfaction than Smokey Joe Wood. In just his fourth full season in the majors, he had scaled the heights of pitching stardom with thirty-seven victories, including three when it mattered most in the postseason.

Accomplishing such a feat was not without cost, however. "I still remember talking to him before one of the Series games and suddenly realizing that he couldn't speak," recalled Harry Hooper. "Couldn't say a word. The strain had gotten too much for him. Well, what do you expect? I think he was only about twenty-two when all this was happening. Mighty young to be under such pressure for so many months."

That pressure would only intensify as Wood and his teammates prepared to defend their championship the following season.

CHAPTER THREE
A ROUGH TRANSITION (1913–1915)

C hange was in the air in 1913. For the first time since 1897, a Democrat was sitting in the White House and the new president was giving every indication that he was ready and eager to shake things up. "We have been proud of our industrial achievements," Woodrow Wilson told the nation in his thoughtful inaugural address of March 4, "but we have not hitherto stopped thoughtfully enough to count the human cost, the cost of lives snuffed out, of energies overtaxed and broken, the fearful physical and spiritual cost to the men and women and children upon whom the dead weight and burden of it all has fallen pitilessly the years through."

To remedy the situation, Wilson embarked on an ambitious program of social, political, and economic reform that sought to empower organized labor, trim the excesses of big business, and expand the rights of ordinary citizens. "We know our task to be no mere task of politics," he said, "but a task which shall search us through and through, whether we be able to understand our time and the need of our people, whether we be indeed their spokesmen and interpreters, whether we have the pure heart to comprehend and the rectified will to choose our high course of action."

Yet this drive for "progressive" change was not emanating from Washington, D.C., alone. Across the land, women seeking their long denied right to vote had organized themselves into an effective political force behind the leadership of Carrie Chapman Catt and Alice Paul. Employing such time-honored protest tactics as mass public rallies, picketing, and outright civil disobedience, they were able to garner widespread attention and support for their cause. The results were impressive. Already nine states, including California, Michigan, Oregon, Colorado, and Arizona, had embraced full suffrage, while several others were actively in the process of doing so. "No longer do we have to go out and drum up people to serve on committees or to sell seats," remarked one proud organizer. "We have a rush of volunteers. We don't have to push the work; we help it along now."

No such feeling of forward movement or reward existed among Boston baseball fans in 1913. In what amounted to an embarrassingly weak defense of their championship crown, the Red Sox slipped to fourth place, an unsightly fifteen-and-a-half games off the pace. While there was plenty of blame to go around, any discussion of the team's fall from grace must begin with Smokey Joe Wood.

A thirty-game winner the year before, the twenty-three-year-old right-hander saw his win total drop to eleven in 1913 following a freak spring training accident that broke the thumb on his right pitching hand. "I went to field a ground ball on wet grass and I slipped and fell on my thumb," Wood later recalled. "It was in a cast for two or three weeks. I don't know whether I tried to pitch too soon after that, or whether something happened to my shoulder at the same time. But whatever it was, I never pitched again without a terrific amount of pain in my right shoulder. Never again."

Although he would lead the league in earned run average (1.49) in 1915 to go with fifteen wins, he was unable to complete a full season for the rest of his career or come close to matching his 1912 level of pitching excellence. "I wasn't the Invincible Joe Wood anymore," he said.

Nor were Wood's teammates on the mound much better. Save for Ray Collins's 19–8 mark, the rest of the starting staff had significant drop-offs from the previous season. In fact, Buck O'Brien and Hugh Bedient, who combined for forty wins in 1912, slumped to less than half that total in 1913. Neither would pitch in the big leagues beyond the 1915 season.

Aside from Wood's arm miseries, the Red Sox were also plagued by ruinous internal club divisions. Interestingly, Wood figured prominently here as well. For he, along with his best friend and roommate Tris Speaker, headed a team clique known as the "Masons," so named because of their fiercely embraced Protestant heritage and outward hostility to the "Knights of Columbus," the name given to the Catholics on the roster. Indeed, Speaker, who once admitted he was a member of the virulently racist Ku Klux Klan organization, had a long-running personal feud with catcher Bill "Rough" Carrigan, a practicing Roman Catholic.

According to Carrigan's son, the personal rift between the two Boston stars was only "settled" when his father challenged Speaker "to a fist fight behind closed doors," a fistfight that Carrigan won. Speaker also had major run-ins with fellow Golden Outfielders Duffy Lewis and Harry Hooper. "Tris didn't speak to Duffy or Harry Hooper a whole season," one clubhouse insider said. "Why? Because they were Catholics and he wasn't. . . . They used to hate each other. Hate each other!"

The sectarian divide mirrored larger social currents taking place within Boston society at the time. Since the late 1840s, sizable numbers of Catholic immigrants, especially Irish Catholics, had come to the Hub in search of greater political freedom and economic opportunity. But the native Protestant inhabitants, or Yankees, as they were called, were not at all welcoming. The latter saw the newcomers as threats to their jobs, religion, and established culture. As the local Catholic population swelled to over 40 percent of the city's population by century's end, so did unease among the Yankees. "To a Yankee like Henry Adams," the political historian Alec Barbrook later observed, it "must have seemed that the dangers of the collapse of the old civilization were very real and unavoidable."

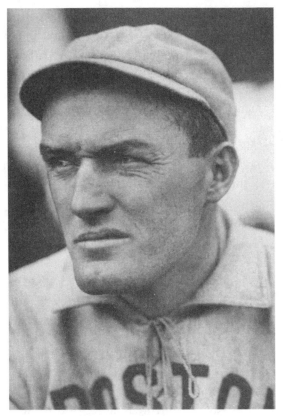

Player-manager Bill "Rough" Carrigan took over an underperforming and badly divided team in 1913 and quickly remolded it into a championship caliber squad over the next two seasons. "He was the greatest manager I ever played for," Babe Ruth later claimed. (Courtesy of the Boston Red Sox.)

With regard to the Red Sox, all this internal discord served to convince team owner James McAleer that manager Jake Stahl had lost control of the ball club and needed to be replaced. But his managerial choice for taking over the squad in the middle of the 1913 season must have come as a shock to many. For assuming the mantle of team leadership was none other than Bill Carrigan, the object of so much scorn by Speaker and the other Masons. Not that it really mattered.

Under Carrigan's deft guidance, the team closed out the disappointing baseball campaign on a winning note, going 40–30 and thereby avoiding the ignominy of a second division finish. "I realized it wasn't going to be easy," Carrigan said. "It never is when you are appointed manager over players with whom you have been associated for years as a private." But the newly appointed field general made a point of playing no favorites and being consistently fair and aboveboard in his dealings with the club. "You must remember the adage of practicing what you preach when you're in that spot," Carrigan explained. "You can't ask players to live up to any rules you didn't follow yourself when you were one of them. I made a few new regulations. The players, as far as I could see, co-operated."

This was hardly surprising. If anyone was born to lead ballplayers and get the most out of them, it was the scrappy grocer's son from Lewiston, Maine. "In my estimation, Bill Carrigan was the greatest manager in Red Sox history," baseball historian Richard A. Johnson maintains. "His influence over the history of the team and the game itself is enormous."

Longtime Carrigan charges like Babe Ruth would not take issue with Johnson over this assessment. "He brought me up and taught me how to be a big league pitcher," Ruth said of Carrigan. "He knew all the hitters in the league and how to pitch to them. Nobody waved off Rough's signs." On the rare occasion anyone did, there were immediate repercussions. "When Carrigan told one of his pitchers to knock a man down and the batter didn't hit the dirt," remembered a rival manager, "the pitcher was fined."

Carrigan earned his tough-guy reputation from his many years laboring behind the plate. While only a lifetime .257 hitter, the stocky five-foot, seven-inch, 170-pound Holy Cross graduate stood out with his pile-driving approach to catching. "I remember one time when we were playing Detroit," Larry Gardner said. "George Moriarty was their third baseman. He and Bill were actually good friends. Moriarty got on first and yelled to Bill, 'Hey, you Irish

SOB,' (the funny thing was Moriarty was Irish, too), 'I'm going to come around the bases and knock you on your arse.'"

As promised, Moriarty did in fact round third base and make a beeline toward home plate. But Carrigan was ready for him. "It was Moriarty, not Bill, that was knocked over," Gardner said. To punctuate his triumph, Carrigan expectorated a stream of tobacco juice upon the now prostrate Detroit star at his feet. "And how do you like that, you Irish SOB?" he said.

For the most part though, Carrigan believed his reputation for brawling was based more on perception than reality. "Except for a brief exchange of swings I engaged in with [Detroit's] Sam Crawford a couple of years after the Moriarty incident, I never got into what you would call a real fight on the field," he claimed. "Oh, I engaged in minor mix-ups. Every player did back there. I'd charge rivals now and then and they'd charge me, but nothing much ever came of it."

What he did excel at was brawling of a "verbal sort," upbraiding opponents and teammates alike if he determined they had crossed him. "I was pretty good at that," he boasted. "In fact, I found it a very valuable weapon when managing."

Away from the dugout, Carrigan was something else: a taciturn and dutiful family man. In fact, one of the main reasons he eventually left the game at the height of his fame and success was to spend more time at home. He had married Beulah Bartlett in 1915 and had started a family. "He got sick of living out of a suitcase," his son Bill Jr. later explained.

But then, family had always come first with Carrigan. As a teenager he had foregone the opportunity of earning a diploma from the elite boys preparatory school Phillips Exeter Academy of New Hampshire when his grocer father suddenly took ill. They "wanted him to come back and help run the store," Bill Jr. said. Not giving the matter a second thought, Carrigan packed his bags and went immediately home. There was a right way to do things and a wrong way. The Lewiston native always strove for the former.

Carrigan initially had mixed feelings about becoming manager of the Red Sox. "I was anything but elated," he later revealed. "I liked Stahl very well, all the players did, and I thought he had done a fine job. In no way could Jake have been held responsible for our lowly position in the race at that time. . . . I tried to point this out to McAleer, but he wouldn't listen." Instead, McAleer bluntly informed him that if he didn't take the job, he would give it to someone else. "So I took the job," Carrigan said. Ironically, it was McAleer himself who would soon be forced into seeking other employment.

Furious that McAleer had bumped one of his closest friends from the Boston managerial post, the always-volatile Ban Johnson sought revenge for this perceived "hasty and ill-advised" move. The AL president used all his considerable influence within league councils to oust McAleer as owner and replace him with a tall self-made millionaire and avid baseball fan named Joseph Lannin.

A native of Quebec, Canada, Lannin had arrived in Boston at age seventeen to work as an office boy. Apparently unsatisfied with his job, Lannin moved on to become a bellboy at a local hotel, where his personal drive and initiative earned him steady promotions and a better situation as a steward at a rival establishment. But Lannin's natural business instincts and burning individual ambition could not hold him there very long. He eventually moved to New York, put together a group of investors, and bought a hotel on Long Island. The venture proved successful and he was able to add extensively to his real estate holdings in the years ahead. Among his many purchases was a minority ownership stake in the Boston Braves, which he divested himself of after Johnson approached him about buying the Red Sox for a reported $200,000.

"It would be no unusual thing for [second baseman and assistant coach Heinie Wagner] and me to go to our apartment in Forest Hills after the theater and find Mr. Lannin waiting to talk baseball with us," Bill Carrigan said. When he wasn't keeping close tabs on his varied business holdings, Lannin liked to play checkers, a game he took up shortly after arriving in Massachusetts. It was in some

Equal parts financial genius and hands-on manager, new Red Sox owner Joseph Lannin always wanted to know how his investments were faring, whether they be his real estate holdings or his ball club. (Courtesy of the Library of Congress.)

ways a perfect outlet for his intense and aggressive personality. "He was soon able to beat the cracker-box philosophers in all the villages around about," observed one journalist. Indeed, Lannin became so adept at checkers that he was actually regarded as a worthy challenger to Christy Mathewson, the uncrowned checkers king of major league baseball.

While no record exists that the two ever squared off for a match, Lannin was once quoted as saying he felt checkers contributed to Mathewson being "one of the brainiest pitchers in this country."

Concomitantly, he probably felt that the same discipline, patience, and strategy required for success in checkers would likewise benefit him when he was conducting his own private business affairs. For sure, Lannin was always looking for a competitive edge, even if it involved huddling for hours over a red and black checker board.

Babe Ruth broke in with the team as a talented yet wildly undisciplined rookie pitching sensation in 1914. He would contribute eighteen wins to Boston's pennant-winning run the following season. (Courtesy of the Boston Red Sox.)

Despite the front-office musical chairs, the Red Sox improved to second place in 1914 with a 91–62 record. Helping account for this dramatic turnaround in the standings were two pitching newcomers: George "Rube" Foster and Hubert "Dutch" Leonard. Obtained from the Texas League late in the 1913 season, Foster proved to be less than sterling in his Boston debut, going 3–4 in ten starts. But things took a major upswing for the diminutive five-foot, seven-inch, 160-pound right-hander in 1914 as his improved command of his fastball produced a 14–8 mark.

Foster would go on to win forty more games as a starter for the Sox over the next three seasons before a sore arm and an unwanted trade to Cincinnati in 1918 forced him to retire from the game. But in his prime, the hard-working Oklahoman was something to behold. He "impressed me as being a mighty sweet pitcher," an opposing manager said.

The same term of endearment easily applied to Leonard. A former collegiate star at St. Mary's College in California, the same school that produced Sox teammates Duffy Lewis and Harry Hooper, Leonard made history in 1914 by compiling a 0.96 ERA, the lowest ever recorded in the annals of major league baseball. Notwithstanding this amazing accomplishment, the moody and petulant lefty was unable to lead the club in wins, as a late season wrist injury dropped him one shy of the twenty victories recorded by teammate Ray Collins. As he was often wont to do, Leonard no doubt consoled himself by picking a fight with someone on the team.

"Leonard, much more worldly-wise than the Babe [Ruth] at the time, delighted in arguing," Carrigan recalled. "He couldn't draw [assistant coach Heinie] Wagner or me into his discussions, but Babe would often fall into the trap. Then the fun would begin. Many a time Heinie and I had to hold them apart to keep them from springing at each other's throat."

Yet beyond these adolescent clubhouse tantrums and record-setting performances, 1914 is best remembered for what happened away from the playing field. In August, Europe exploded into all-out war pitting the Allies (Great Britain, France, and Russia) against the Central Powers (Germany, Austria-Hungary, and Turkey). The precipitating incident was the assassination of Archduke Franz Ferdinand, heir to the Austro-Hungarian throne, by a Serbian terrorist on June 18 in Sarajevo, Bosnia. The murder "proved to be the pretext for the delicately balanced alliance system of the great powers to crumble into world-wide war," notes historian John Milton Cooper. It also meant the end of La Belle Époque, an era when general peace, economic prosperity, and an unabashed belief in human progress ruled the Continent. "The lamps are going out all over Europe," lamented British Foreign Secretary Sir Edward Gray. "We shall not see them relit again in our lifetime."

While the United States had the luxury of standing aloof from "the dreadful conflict," thanks to the protective geographic barrier of the Atlantic Ocean, there were nevertheless strong fears that this "splendid isolation" would not last. "It would be an irony of fate if my administration had to deal chiefly with foreign affairs," President Woodrow Wilson remarked. To keep such disturbing thoughts at bay, many Americans tried to distract themselves by focusing on frivolous mass entertainments like long-distance automobile races, the emerging motion picture industry, and, of course, baseball.

Regarding the latter, perhaps no individual was better equipped to capture the popular imagination than a rookie Boston pitching sensation by the name of George Herman "Babe" Ruth. Just nineteen and fresh out of reform school, Ruth was like an unbridled colt bursting with energy. "I was a kid with a healthy appetite and a zest for life," he later wrote. "Life looked like a great big lark to me."

An unapologetic satyr, he ate, drank, and partied to excess while failing to display anything remotely resembling good personal hygiene. In fact, it was commonplace for the uninhibited left-hander to neglect changing his sweaty underwear after a game. This disgusting habit drew incredulous gasps from his teammates, who began calling him "the Big Baboon" behind his back.

One teammate in particular who took a strong exception to Ruth was Smokey Joe Wood. During a pregame warm-up one afternoon among the team's pitchers, Ruth playfully made a half-hearted effort to field a ball that got away from Wood's catcher. "It didn't amount to much," Ruth recalled, "but Wood yelled something at me and I yelled something back." Before either of them knew it, they were both purposely striding toward the clubhouse looking to settle their dispute with fists. Only the timely intervention of manager Bill Carrigan prevented the incident from escalating into violence.

There was no love lost between Ruth and Wood, or by extension Smokey Joe's closest friend and fellow Mason Tris Speaker. The fact that Ruth was a practicing Catholic was bad enough, but the way he had confronted Wood left a reservoir of "bad will" between himself and Speaker. For his part, Ruth later tried to downplay their personal differences and made no mention of the religious angle. Speaker "was Joe's pal," he explained diplomatically, "naturally he was on Wood's side."

Harder to dismiss was the "rough treatment" that Ruth received after he took batting practice one day. Returning to the ballpark the following afternoon, he discovered that his bats had been "neatly sawed in two." Whether it was Speaker or Wood or any of the other Masons on the team who performed the actual deed is open to speculation. But it is clear that Ruth was not warmly embraced by a large segment of the Boston locker room.

None of this really mattered to the easygoing Ruth, however. He was having too much fun outside the ballpark to especially care. "He was one of a kind," offered Waite Hoyt, his future Hall of Fame teammate on the New York Yankees. "If he had never played ball, if you had never heard of him and passed him on Broadway, you'd turn around and look."

A notoriously light sleeper and carouser, Ruth liked to spend his evenings at home or on the road seeking the company of prostitutes. Once during a routine police inspection of a suspected brothel in Detroit, an officer discovered Ruth traveling down a flight of stairs "with a nude girl on his shoulders" and singing "Oh what a gal! Oh what a pal!" In what would become an all-too-familiar pattern in his life, Ruth and his boisterous party mates got off scot-free. "I agreed to let the fun go on as long as Ruth was in town," the bemused officer said.

Nothing was seemingly off limits to Ruth: excessive booze, high-stakes gambling, passing gas indiscriminately in public, or munching on a bag of peanuts while having sex. Not even an impulsive early marriage to a pretty if emotionally fragile coffee shop waitress named Helen Woodford when he first arrived in Boston could temper his behavior. If anything, his "bad boy" antics grew worse. As Ruth's entertainingly discerning biographer Leigh Montville writes, "They would do things together, be seen in public, go to bowling parties and events, but he clearly had an outside paper route too, one that did not include her. Very early there was an accommodation for infidelities."

Although Ruth and Helen remained officially married until she died in a tragic house fire in 1929, they had both been leading essentially separate lives for several years. In fact, at the time of her death, Helen had been living with a Watertown, Massachusetts, dentist named Edward H. Kinder, who everyone in her immediate neighborhood assumed was her real husband.

"You know," Harry Hooper later told the historian Lawrence S. Ritter, "I saw it all happen, from beginning to end. But sometimes I still can't believe what I saw: this nineteen-year-old kid, crude, poorly educated, only lightly brushed by the social veneer we call civilization, gradually transformed into the idol of American youth and the symbol of baseball the world over—a man loved by more people and with an intensity of feeling that perhaps has never been equaled before or since. I saw a man transformed into something pretty close to a god. If somebody had predicted that back on the Boston Red Sox in 1914, he would have been thrown into a lunatic asylum."

Ruth's unlikely path to baseball divinity began in the rough-and-tumble waterfront district of Baltimore, Maryland, where he was born on February 6, 1895. His parents operated a popular saloon in the area and consequently had little time for their rambunctious son, who always seemed to be getting into trouble with the law. "Looking back on my boyhood," he once confessed, "I honestly don't remember being aware of the difference between right and wrong."

His surroundings didn't help. The saloon became his home, schoolhouse, and playground all rolled into one. It was hardly a nurturing environment. "When I wasn't living over it," Ruth later recalled, "I was living in it, studying the rough talk of the longshoremen, merchant sailors, roustabouts and waterfront bums. . . . I had a rotten start and it took me a long time to get my bearings."

Unable to tame his wildly boisterous nature, Ruth's parents essentially threw in the towel and turned custody of him over to the St. Mary's Industrial School for Boys, a local Catholic-run reform school. There he met the man who would dramatically change his life: Brother Matthias Boutlier. A tall, authoritative figure who served as the school's prefect of discipline, Brother Matthias commanded the instant respect and attention of troubled kids like Ruth. "He was the father I needed," Ruth said. "He taught me to read and write—and he taught me the difference between right and wrong."

Equally important, Brother Matthias introduced Ruth to baseball, patiently instructing him on the fundamentals of the game, including how to swing a bat. "The baseball of that time was a lump of mush," Ruth said. "But Brother Matthias would stand at the end of the yard, a finger mitt on his left hand and a bat in his right, toss the ball up with his left hand and give it a terrific belt with the bat he held in his right hand. When he felt like it, he could hit it a little harder and make the ball clear the fence in center field. The ball would have to carry at least 350 feet, a terrific knock in those days and a real sock—in view of the fact it was hit with one hand—even today. I would stand there and watch him, bug-eyed."

A similar sense of awe gripped observers who witnessed Ruth playing ball as a teenager. Already a strapping six-footer with matchless athletic grace, he became "the absolute king of St. Mary's baseball," averaging close to .500 at the plate and throwing bullets from the mound. Indeed, in one contest during his final season with St. Mary's, he fanned twenty-two batters. Clearly, he was destined for bigger and better things.

At least that was the impression of Jack Dunn, the minor league owner and manager of the Baltimore Orioles of the International League. Dunn had been tipped off about Ruth's unique abilities and decided to venture to St. Mary's to personally check him out. He obviously liked what he saw as he signed the youngster to a $600 professional contract to pitch for the 1914 season. "You'll make it, Babe," Brother Matthias assured Ruth upon parting.

As always when it came to Ruth, the discerning cleric knew what he was talking about. By midseason, Ruth had reeled off fourteen wins on the hill for the Orioles, drawing widespread praise and attention from big-league clubs. "Whenever you're ready to put him on the market," New York Giants skipper John McGraw reportedly told Dunn, "I want you to give me first crack at him." Unfortunately for McGraw, he never got the opportunity.

Dunn, who enjoyed a close personal relationship with Connie Mack, decided to give the Philadelphia Athletics owner and manager that special privilege along with the signing rights to pitcher Ernie Shore and catch Ben Egan. But to his everlasting regret, Mack declined, citing a lack of funds. "I'd like to have those fellows but I can't afford them, Jack," Mack said. "You'd better peddle them to some other club that has more money than I have to get the best price for them."

Enter Joseph Lannin. Frustrated by his club's also-ran status to the Athletics in the AL standings, the opportunistic Red Sox magnate swooped in to make the deal. In return for Ruth, Shore, and Egan, Dunn received $22,500, a fairly large sum of money in 1914 and an amount that allowed the financially strapped Baltimore owner to remain in business. "It was a hard blow to me to be forced to wreck the splendid team I had," he explained, "but nobody is willing to come across if I go broke."

Although Ruth's arrival did not result in Boston overtaking Philadelphia for the league championship in 1914, he did give tantalizing hints of things to come. In his Red Sox pitching debut against Cleveland on July 11, Ruth lasted seven innings and came away with a 4–3 victory.

"If I remember," Bill Carrigan recalled, "Babe was crude in spots. Every so often he served up a fat pitch or a bad pitch, when he shouldn't have. But he showed plenty of baseball 'savvy.' He picked a runner off third base. He also cut off a throw from the outfield and threw out a runner at second. Anybody could see he'd quickly develop into a standout with a little more experience. He had a barrel of stuff, his speed was blinding and his ball was alive."

In his real-time account of the game, T. H. Murnane of the *Boston Globe* confirmed Carrigan's overall positive assessment: Ruth "has a natural delivery, fine control and a curve ball that bothers the batsman, but he has room for improvement and will undoubtedly become a fine pitcher under the care of Manager Carrigan."

Ruth would go on to post an 18–8 record in 1915 and be a major factor in Boston's triumphant return to the World Series that October. But he was not the only newcomer injecting talent and energy into the Olde Towne Team. Ernie Shore, the six-foot, four-inch, 220-pound right-hander from North Carolina who came over with Ruth in the Baltimore transaction, had an even better year, finishing 19–8 with a 1.64 ERA in 247 innings pitched.

"A lot of my career was tied with the Babe," he later told the writer Donald Honig. "We were always good friends, Babe and myself. He was always a larger-than-life sort of fellow, even way back when." So close did the young hurlers become that it was reported Ruth frequently made use of Shore's toothbrush without the latter's permission. Shore later denied the accuracy of this account. "It was my shaving brush," he corrected.

"My particular stock in trade is a fastball which I have trained so that it has a peculiar break," he told *Baseball Magazine* in 1917. "The average fastball will shoot to one side or the other as it crosses the

Ernie Shore was one of the fiercest competitors to ever take the mound for the Sox. From 1914 to 1917 Shore averaged sixteen wins a season for the team while consistently holding opponents to a scant two runs per game. (Courtesy of the Boston Red Sox.)

plate, and in some cases where thrown with sufficient speed, will actually rise. My fast ball, on the other hand, drops sharply. It will not break as much as a curve, but the drop will be much more sudden."

Another emerging player who made a significant contribution in 1915 was infielder Everett "Deacon" Scott, a light hitting five-foot, seven-inch, 148-pound shortstop from Bluffton, Indiana, who more

CHAPTER THREE

than made up for his deficiencies at the plate with his steady glove work. In his thirteen years in the bigs, the mild-mannered Scott led the league in fielding percentage at his position thirteen times. In 1915, he was already considered one of the finest defensive performers in the game, exhibiting sure hands and great range as the ex officio leader of the Red Sox infield.

"He made few errors, played batters like a psychic, and threw quickly with unfailing accuracy," notes the writer Leo Trachtenberg. Scott also became a model of durability, playing in 1,307 consecutive games from 1916 to 1925, a major league milestone that only Hall of Famers Lou Gehrig and Cal Ripken Jr. have been able to surpass. "I started game after game because my manager thought I was helping the team, not because I had a consecutive streak going," he said.

Even with the infusion of youth, the Red Sox got off to a mediocre start in 1915. They were hovering around the .500 mark and mired in third place as nagging injuries to starting pitchers Dutch Leonard and Smokey Joe Wood and the lack of a quality defensive second baseman all took their toll. Things did manage to pick up again for the team in early July, however, when Lannin pulled out his checkbook to acquire accomplished Athletics infielder Jack Barry for $8,000.

The deal came about thanks to an unexpected series of events going back to the preceding fall's World Series, when the "Miracle" Boston Braves of Hall of Fame shortstop Walter James "Rabbit" Maranville disposed of Connie Mack's heavily favored club in four straight games. Angered by the humiliating loss, Mack determined that the time was right to break up his aging squad, which had won four of the previous five AL flags.

So in addition to Barry, out the door went such long-standing A's stars as Eddie Collins, Frank "Home Run" Baker, Jack Coombs, Charles "Chief" Bender, and Eddie Plank. Declining gate receipts and an established aversion on Mack's part to paying fair market wages to his standout veteran performers no doubt also influenced his decision. "Champions cost money," Mack later groused. As a

84

result, the Athletics would finish in last place in 1915 and not climb out of the second division until a decade later.

Though he had spent the majority of his playing time as a shortstop with Philadelphia, Barry offered no strong objections when Carrigan saw fit to move him over to second upon his arrival in Boston. At this stage in his career, the businesslike veteran actually welcomed the change. "He considered [second base] a snap compared to shortstop," his biographer John McMurray writes. Besides, Boston's outgoing starting second baseman, the fading Heinie Wagner, had just come to the end of the line as a player.

Barry would thus be plugging a major defensive hole in the middle of the Sox infield while complementing the tried and true talents of Everett Scott at short and Larry Gardner at third base. First base was split between Dick Hoblitzell and Del Gainor, two capable pros who hit .283 and .295 respectively in 1915. It was a win-win proposition for everybody concerned. Accordingly, the team was able to storm back into contention and seize first place by mid-July. But nipping at their heels was an exceptionally fine Detroit Tigers ball club led by Ty Cobb.

Having last played in a World Series in 1909, the combative "Georgia Peach" was eager to get another shot at a championship. Cobb, whom most of his contemporaries viewed with grudging respect if not admiration, was perhaps the greatest player of the Deadball Era. Apart from routinely posting batting averages of .350 or better, the speedy slap hitter displayed a ferocious, some might even argue psychotic, will to win. "I was like a steel spring with a growing and dangerous flaw in it," he once confessed. "If it is wound too tight or has the slightest weak point, the spring will fly apart and then it is done for."

Neither Cobb nor the Tigers seemed done for as they battled the Red Sox down the stretch in 1915. Both teams remained close to one another until late September, when Boston took three out of four from the Tigers at home. Ruth did his part in the fourth and final contest, going seven and two-thirds innings in a 3–2 victory over

Second baseman Jack Barry (third from left) conversing with teammates Babe Ruth, Bill Carrigan, and Vean Gregg. His mid-season acquisition from the Philadelphia Athletics in 1915 helped fill a major defensive hole in the Boston infield. (Courtesy of the Library of Congress.)

George "Hooks" Dauss, a twenty-four-game winner in 1915 and Detroit's right-handed staff ace. "Manager Carrigan took a chance on 'Babe' Ruth, and but for his temporary wildness in the first inning [when he gave up all of Detroit's runs on a two-run single by outfielder Bobby Veach], he would have pulled through without the least doubt," the *Boston Globe* reported.

While such clutch performances would have endeared any player to his hometown fans, no such inducements were necessary in Ruth's case. He had already become a major Boston celebrity and center of attention. "We'd come out on the field to warm up and you could hear them all over the park: 'Babe, hey Babe,'" Shore remembered. "And he'd always turn around and wave and give them that big smile. They loved him and he loved them. That was the secret of the Babe Ruth magic—genuine feeling on both sides. It wasn't ego with the Babe; never say that. It was just the sheer joy of being on a ball field and relating to people. That was his gift, as much as hitting home runs."

Ruth's win pushed the Tigers four games back in the standings and essentially guaranteed the pennant for Boston, which finished the season with a major league best 101–50 mark. But to those closely following the club, the team's victory had to be considered as much a testament to Tris Speaker's sustained excellence on the diamond as to anything else. For despite seeing his batting average and RBIs dip to .322 and sixty-nine respectively from .338 and ninety showings the previous year, the twenty-seven-year-old outfielder was still very much at the apex of his career, one that would stretch a full twenty-two seasons and eventually earn him a bronze plaque in Cooperstown.

"In my opinion," former Boston teammate Marty McHale once said, "he was the greatest of all outfielders, and second only to [Ty] Cobb in all-around ability." The record book bears out this assertion. Speaker was a lifetime .344 hitter who led the league in putouts seven times while compiling an amazing 139 career double plays. To put the latter statistic in proper perspective, Willie Mays, considered by most baseball fans and writers to be the greatest outfielder in history, could manage only sixty double plays in twenty-two seasons.

"He was more than a great outfielder; he actually was a fifth infielder," Babe Ruth later said. "Tris would play close and get many balls in short center or right field and occasionally throw a runner out at first. Maybe with the present lively ball Tris couldn't play that way. But he could go out for them, and with the modern ball his hitting would be much greater."

Tellingly, the supremely self-confident star never disputed claims made about his baseball greatness, howsoever hyperbolic or obsequious they sometimes were. He frankly regarded himself as being among the elite players of his era, perhaps even of all time. Yet he was not shy about giving credit where credit was due, especially to those who helped him early on in his career, people like Hall of Famer Cy Young.

"The old fellow took a fancy to me, and said he would make a slick outfielder of me," Speaker recalled. "He'd take me out on the practice field and hit fungos to me by the hour. I got to watching, and studying his fungo swing, and by doing that I could start after the ball before he actually hit it."

These practice sessions later proved invaluable when Speaker became the regular Boston center fielder. "By closely observing the batsman at the plate, after he had reached a certain arc in his swing," he said, "I could also gauge the power of the swing. In that way I got the jump on the ball."

The son of a farmer, Speaker spent his youth in the rugged "cow country" of eastern Texas in the late 1800s, helping out on the family homestead and raising apprehension among neighbors with his avid interest in firearms. "When he wasn't much more'n twelve years old, he packed a six-shooter as big as he was," recalled one acquaintance from this period. "Used to worry the life out of the town marshal, but I never heard of him getting into any real scrapes. Just a lot of mischief like kids sort of stumble into when they've got more energy than they know what to do with."

Being a southerner with relatives who had fought on the Confederate side in the Civil War, or the "War of Northern Aggression," as many of his peers preferred to call it, Speaker had a natural edge about him. He was abrupt, quarrelsome, and often contemptuous in his dealings with others, especially if they were non-southerners. It was his way or the highway, thereby precluding the need for any sort of compromise or meaningful personal dialogue. This extended to matters on the baseball diamond. Once, when he was moved from his customary third spot in the team batting order to leadoff, he loudly announced his unhappiness in the strongest of terms. "That will be all of that stuff, or else," he exclaimed in his trademark snarling, threatening tone.

In later years, he never tired of defending the "Lost Cause," that unique American myth that states the pro-slavery South was justified, perhaps even divinely sanctioned, in waging its treasonous war against the Union and the federal government. In truth, Speaker was an unapologetic Confederate's Confederate, as demonstrated by his self-admitted membership in the Ku Klux Klan. He "would have preferred to play only with young men like him, white Anglo-Saxon Protestants from below the Mason-Dixon line," his biographer Timothy M. Gay notes.

As a boy, Speaker was able to channel this aggressive energy toward playing baseball. But while he was a clear standout on his high school team, he wasn't exactly bowled over with lucrative offers to turn pro upon graduation. After signing on to play for the minor North Texas League for $65 a month in 1906, Speaker was able to catch the eye of the Red Sox, who signed him up for the 1907 season. He wasn't able to stick around the parent club for long, however. He batted an unimpressive .158 and was promptly released.

Undaunted, Speaker attempted hooking up with the New York Giants the following season, but he was bluntly told by manager John McGraw to look elsewhere. "I did everything I could, but I couldn't get him to change his mind," Speaker later said. With his options nearly run out, he agreed to play for the Little Rock, Arkansas, franchise in the Southern League and surprised everyone by hitting .350

for the 1908 campaign. Now inquiries came pouring in from the majors pertaining to his availability as an outfielder. "But back to the Red Sox I went," Speaker said. And there he would remain as an integral member of the team until departing for Cleveland in 1916.

The same doggedness which Speaker exhibited in getting to the big leagues would also serve him well when it came to negotiating his salary. In an era where baseball owners held all the financial leverage thanks to the constrictive reserve clause, players like Speaker were expected to passively accept the terms of whatever contract they were tendered by team management. Yet Speaker refused to play along. If he felt he deserved a higher salary than the front office was willing to give, he was not afraid of holding out.

Such displays of personal independence only gained weight when the Federal League began formal operations in 1914. A third major league that was established by a group of well-heeled busi-

A lifetime .344 hitter and outstanding outfielder, Tris Speaker played with a proverbial chip on his shoulder. However, all this pent-up anger did not prevent him from pacing the Red Sox to two World Series championships. (Courtesy of the Library of Congress.)

ness people to break the monopolistic hold that the American and National Leagues had long exercised over the game, the "Feds" were an economic force to be reckoned with. They set up shop in eight major metropolitan centers, including Chicago, Brooklyn, St. Louis, and Pittsburgh, and were willing to pay top dollar for proven stars like Speaker.

In truth, representatives from the Brooklyn Feds had offered Speaker $18,000 to sign immediately with the team for the 1915 season. Cagily, Speaker asked for more time to assess the situation and then relayed the Feds' proposition to Joseph Lannin. With the onus now squarely on his shoulders, the savvy Red Sox owner felt compelled to match these salary terms by drawing up a new two-year, $36,000 deal that was "larger than any heretofore paid a player." It was either that or risk losing his star outfielder to an enterprising new rival that was out to supplant him and his league. This was simply something Lannin was unwilling to permit. Speaker thus re-signed with the Sox and could not have been happier.

"I'm delighted to be . . . on the Boston payroll again," he beamed. "The Red Sox are a great team, Boston is a great ball town, and it goes without saying that Manager Carrigan will surely have the best that is in me at all times." Speaker's grit and determination had paid off handsomely once again, this time with a substantial financial windfall. But forebodingly, not everyone came away as pleased with the outcome. "What did I get myself into?" Lannin complained afterward.

Facing the Red Sox in the World Series were the upstart Philadelphia Phillies. Perennial bottom feeders since their franchise founding in 1883, the Phillies shocked the baseball world by winning ninety games and taking the NL flag by seven games. Hall of Fame right-hander Grover Cleveland Alexander proved to be the straw that stirred the drink here. In forty-two games he started, he won thirty-one of the decisions while dropping only ten. In addition, he struck out a league best 241 batters while shutting out opponents twelve times with a 1.22 ERA.

"He was one of the first pitchers to throw what they call a slider today," Ernie Shore told historian Donald Honig in 1979. "He threw a live fastball too, and had good control. The Philadelphia papers were filled with praise for him. He was their ace and they were very proud of him and were counting on him. They called him Alexander the Great, and he surely was a great one."

Away from the mound, Alexander, who suffered from epilepsy, was far less impressive. He was a full-fledged alcoholic who found himself reduced to performing in a New York flea circus for income when his playing days were over. But when he was in his prime, as he was in 1915, few could match his skill at getting batters out. As one writer recalled, "He not only could pinpoint the fast ball and curve, low and away, but he also had the knack of taking something off his fast one by degrees and he came up with a screwball about which little has been written. He also threw deceptively."

After Alexander, there was a significant drop-off in terms of the overall quality in the Phillies' pitching rotation, although Georgia native and right-handed side-armer Erskine Mayer did produce a 21–15 record in 274 innings of work. As *Baseball Magazine* observed, "Mayer is the man on the Phillies' staff who has borne most of the burden of the club not carried by the broad shoulders of Alexander."

Philadelphia hit .247 as a team with slugging outfielder Gavvy "Cactus" Cravath providing most of the offensive thunder. He thumped twenty-four homers, up to that point the most recorded by a major leaguer in a single season since the turn of the century. The thirty-four-year-old Cravath, who had spent the better part of a decade languishing in the minors, did not become a regular in the majors until 1912, when he hit .284 in 130 games for the Phillies. He would go on to have several more productive seasons at the plate, including a NL-leading 128 RBIs in 1913. Yet he would never win a lot of respect for his defensive play in the outfield. "Cravath will save no games by fine ground covering or great throwing," sniffed the *Boston Globe*.

After being delayed several days due to inclement weather, the World Series finally got under way on October 8. Alexander the

Great managed to stifle Boston's offense by striking out six and scattering eight hits in a complete game, 3–1 victory before a home-field crowd of nineteen thousand at Philadelphia's Baker Bowl.

"To him should be given most of the credit for winning the first game of this year's classic," declared a clearly impressed Ty Cobb, who was covering the series for the *Boston Post*. Indeed, despite a self-described case of opening game jitters, in which Boston batters recorded a hit in each of the first eight innings, Alexander was able to pitch his way out of trouble and deliver a signature performance.

The lone exception came in the top of the eighth inning, when he inexplicably walked Speaker on four straight pitches and gave up a run-scoring single to Duffy Lewis. "He didn't seem to have his usual repertoire, and looked not like the three-hit marvel of the season," reported William A. Phelon of *Baseball Magazine*, "but like just a good, game pitcher doing his best without much to do it with."

Boston starter Ernie Shore rose to the occasion, in some ways pitching an even better game than Alexander. In eight full innings, he gave up only five hits, the vast majority of them never leaving the slippery infield. "The wet and soggy condition of the infield was the big determining factor," Carrigan said. "Had the field been dry, none of the four hits the Quakers got would have been possible, and the whole country tonight would be talking about the wonderful game that Shore pitched."

Though he never explicitly used the bad field conditions as an excuse, Shore never disavowed they were a factor in his loss either. "Alexander said after the game that I pitched in hard luck, that the breaks went against me," Shore said. "Well, he was right about that."

Shore's first brush with "hard luck" occurred in the fourth inning, when Philly's George Whitted's slow roller to second allowed teammate Dode Paskert to break home for the first recorded run of the Series. Paskert, an outfielder who hit .244 on the season, had earlier reached base on a dying fly to right field that dropped in for a base hit. While no doubt frustrating, the improbable run hardly appeared to have an effect on Shore, who set down the Phillie batters with mechanical precision over the next three innings.

It was only in the eighth that things really started to get rough for the Boston right-hander. After issuing a one-out walk to weak-hitting infielder Milt Stock, he induced Philadelphia's Dave Bancroft to hit a hard liner at Sox infielder Jack Barry, who played the ball perfectly on the hop while looking for the easy force out at second. "But [shortstop] Everett Scott didn't cover second base, to this day I don't know why," Shore said. "Maybe he didn't think Barry would get it. When Barry wheeled to throw to the base, nobody was there, and he held the ball just long enough for Bancroft to beat it out."

Feeling a bit snake-bitten and not a little frustrated, Shore walked the next Phillies batter to load up the bases for the always dangerous Cravath. "If I tell you that Cravath hit more home runs that year than most *teams* did, you'll get the idea of what kind of slugger he was," Shore said. Cravath didn't hit any long balls on this occasion, but he did drive in the game's go-ahead run on a "high-bounding" ground ball.

Philadelphia added an insurance run when first baseman Fred Luderus, who was slotted after Cravath in the Phillies' lineup, bounced a playable grounder right at Shore. Shore, however, managed to muff the ball after his legs gave out from under him on the wet turf. "All I could do was sit there and watch that little white ball roll away—so slowly I could see each stitch—while the run crossed the plate," he said. "Talk about bad luck. I should have been out of that inning without a run scored. You put their hits end to end and they still wouldn't reach the outfield grass."

Boston's fortunes improved dramatically in game 2 as Rube Foster three-hit the Phillies in a spirit-lifting 2–1 triumph that also saw the diminutive right-hander collect three hits at the plate, including the game-winner in the ninth. "When the battle began little George Foster was merely a Boston pitcher," wrote the *Boston Post*'s Paul Shannon. "Tonight he looms as one of the illustrious figures of world's series strife and over the country flashes the tale of his brilliant achievement."

Carrigan did not disagree. "[Foster] may have twirled a no-hit game or so before he came up to the majors but he never equaled his performance of today," he enthused. "When a man can hold such a team of hitters as the Phillies to three hits in nine innings, in a game where so much is hanging upon the result, I think it proves his class."

Foster demonstrated his mastery from the outset as he retired the first twelve Philadelphia batters he faced, five of them on strike-outs. Despite the domination, the Phillies did break through for a run in the bottom of the fifth when Luderus doubled home Cravath, who had led off the inning with his own two-bagger. That run managed to tie the game 1–1 as Boston had gotten on the scoreboard in the first inning, courtesy of a double steal.

Phillies starter Erskine Mayer, who struck out seven in an otherwise undistinguished outing, had started the game walking Harry Hooper. The Boston outfielder then advanced to third on a base hit by Speaker. With runners at the corners, Carrigan thought the moment was ripe for a little chicanery. He ordered the double steal, but the Phillies were not fooled. Speaker was easily gunned down at second, and Hooper seemed all but assured of a similar fate on the return throw home—that is, until Philly catcher Ed Burns fumbled the ball. "We got a lucky break," Carrigan explained afterward.

That 1–1 score remained intact until the ninth, when Foster drove in Larry Gardner with a well-stroked single to right field to secure the contest for Boston and tie the Series at a game apiece. "It was a Foster day," proclaimed the *Boston Globe*, "and the gamest kid in the big league was there four ways from the center with bells on."

While most of the twenty thousand in attendance were no doubt disappointed by the final score, there was at least one out-of-town fan positively beaming. President Woodrow Wilson, a former amateur baseball player and enthusiastic AL supporter, had made a point of putting aside his official duties to take in the game and throw out the ceremonial first pitch, the first chief executive to do so in the Fall Classic. "I told you so," he reportedly exclaimed to his fiancée Edith Galt at the conclusion of the contest. Galt, a Phillies fan, feigned disapproval. She vowed her team would come back the next game. "You know a woman always has the last word," she said.

Luckily for the Red Sox, Galt's prediction didn't come to pass when they returned home to Boston for game 3. The Sox beat Philadelphia 2–1 in front of a record major league audience of forty-two thousand at Braves Field. That's right, Braves Field. Prior to the Series, Sox owner Joseph Lannin had wisely decided to make the venue shift from Fenway, which could hold only thirty-five thousand spectators, to the larger new ballpark of their longtime NL rivals. The idea here was to keep the turnstiles clicking and accommodate the sure to be massive Series home crowd. Remembered Ernie Shore, "Some of our fans grumbled about not having the games at Fenway, but the players were happy about it because more tickets would be sold and we shared in the receipts. After all, baseball was a business."

Of course, the switch was also not without some ancillary benefits from a competition standpoint. "At the time," notes writer Frederick G. Lieb, "they hadn't moved in the distant Braves Field fences and the National League ball park was an outfielders' paradise

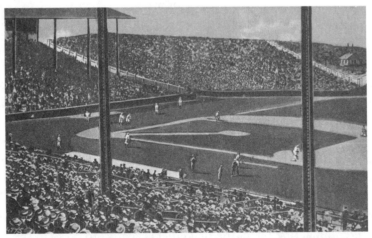

Team management decided to leave the friendly confines of Fenway Park for the newer and more spacious Braves Field for the 1915 World Series. (Courtesy of the Boston Public Library Print Department, Sports Temples of Boston Collection.)

which the great Red Sox trio [of Lewis, Speaker, and Hooper] really could roam and show itself to its best advantage."

Be that as it may, the Phillies came into the contest brimming with confidence. They had good reason to be so self-assured. On the mound for them was their incomparable ace, Alexander, who was just itching to record his second Series victory in only four days. He "was selected to take the measure of [the Sox] and it was freely predicted by the National League sympathizers that this great box artist would certainly defeat the home team," said the *Boston Globe*.

But opposing him was an equally confident Dutch Leonard, who would go on to reward his manager's faith for putting him in such a crucial situation by allowing but three Phillie hits the entire afternoon. "Leonard pitched his greatest game of the year, fully as effective a one as Foster did [the previous game]," Carrigan lauded.

Even so, the Phillies managed to get on the scoreboard first, when Dave Bancroft drove in teammate Ed Burns on a single to center in the top of the third. But the Red Sox were quick to respond in their half of the frame. After Speaker cracked a one-out triple that fell just within the right-field foul line, Sox first baseman Dick Hoblitzell brought him home on a sacrifice fly to center. So personally distraught was Alexander over giving up the extra base hit to Speaker, he felt compelled to visit the Sox clubhouse after the game. "Well, you got me today," he told Speaker.

As clutch a hit as Speaker's triple was, however, it only served to tie the game. The winning tally would not cross the plate until the ninth, when Duffy Lewis plastered an Alexander fastball through the middle of the Phillie infield for a base hit that scored Hooper from third. To say that the "Quaker players" were deeply chagrined by the final result would be an understatement.

As the *Globe* gleefully observed, the Phillies, "with Alexander in the lead, strode from the field, a much-surprised and disappointed lot of ballplayers; for their one great pitcher had been outpointed by one of the Boston youngsters."

Yet overlooked, as he often was in Boston's victories, was Duffy Lewis. Apart from providing the winning hit in game 3, the intense but likable Californian was also wielding an extremely hot bat. In twelve plate appearances to date in the Series, he was hitting a robust .500 to go with a team-leading six total bases. "Duffy Lewis is a man who gets one-tenth the publicity which Babe Ruth does," Walter Johnson once commented. "But the players all recognize him as one of the greatest hitters in the game. He can hit anything and is doubly dangerous in the pinch."

Lewis had entered professional ball in 1907, signing on with the Alameda club of the California State League. While his physique was decidedly nonathletic—he was once referred to as "chunky little Duffy"—the moon-faced five-foot, ten-inch, 170-pound left fielder possessed surprising agility, in addition to an ability to hit the ball a country mile.

He made a big splash in his rookie campaign with Boston in 1910, hitting .283 and finishing second in the league in homers with eight. Many more fine offensive years followed, but it was his spell-binding ability to track down fly balls and throw out runners with unerring accuracy that earned him everlasting fame alongside teammates Tris Speaker and Harry Hooper in the "Golden Outfield," arguably the greatest collection of defensive outfield talent in baseball history. As Connie Mack ruefully noted, "A single that goes through to the outfield should score any man from second. But that doesn't go when we play Boston. It takes a double to bring a man home."

"We used to gang up on a hitter, that's why they had such a hard time hitting one which we couldn't get," Lewis said. "Hooper and I watched Spoke. If he moved to the right we moved to the right. If he moved in, or out, or to the left, we followed him. The pitcher would then take a look around to see where we were, and also Bill Carrigan, who was our manager and catcher. We always knew what the pitcher [was] going to throw because the shortstop always gave us the sign."

"But," as Lewis explained, "the sign came only after Speaker made his move. We never moved once the sign was given, because we didn't want to tip our mitt. Sometimes we'd have to break back the way we had come, but knowing the batter and the pitch and everything, we usually knew it beforehand." He added, "Boy, how we used to gang up on 'em."

Still, being part of such a renowned trio had its drawbacks. "Were the Californian a member of any other outfield in the country," speculated *Baseball Magazine*, "he would be hailed as the wonder of wonders. Because he is a link with the inimitable Hooper and the incomparable Speaker his brilliancy is less discernable." If Lewis was ever bothered by such public oversight, he never let on. Instead, he quietly and effectively went about his business of helping Boston win. "Baseball was very good to me and I love the game," he once said.

An exceptionally patient man with a long fuse when it came to losing his temper, Lewis nevertheless was no pushover. This latter fact was certainly the case when Speaker orchestrated a mean-spirited prank against him one afternoon in Boston. Lewis had recently suffered massive hair loss and was understandably touchy about displaying his bald head in public. Knowing this, Speaker had gotten into the habit of snatching Lewis's uniform cap before games on the field, thus drawing the amused attention of the crowd in the stands. Finally, Lewis had had enough. On this particular day, he warned Speaker he would "kill" him if tried to repeat the same stunt. Unimpressed, Speaker did just that and paid a terrible price. "Duffy showed how serious he was by slamming his bat across Speaker's shin so hard that he had to be taken from the field," noted the writer Ed Linn.

While not a partier of the same caliber as Ruth, Lewis was not against having a good time, especially after he completed a short if undistinguished stint as a performer on the vaudeville circuit following the Series. His act, which was designed to cash in on his Series fame, consisted of his fielding baseball questions from the audience in his Red Sox uniform while trying hard not to look ill at ease.

"Fine and dandy," as one reviewer said of Lewis's show, best describes the blowout party that Lewis threw for himself and his fellow stage acts shortly before wrapping up his stage gig. "Burgundy

Following his impressive performance in the 1915 Series, Duffy Lewis took to the vaudeville stage to cash in on his newfound celebrity. "If Duffy can be persuaded to talk a little louder, so that the fans in the gallery can understand," wrote one sympathetic newspaper reviewer, "everything will be fine and dandy." (Courtesy of the Library of Congress.)

flowed like water," he remembered. "A group of acrobats who tossed each other around like yo-yos opened the show. Well, you should have seen them at the last night's performance after my dinner. Luckily for them they had a net below, because they missed every time they were tossed from one trapeze to the other. After the show the theater manager came to my dressing room and said, 'Lewis, I'm glad [you are] through. You've disrupted show business.'"

When the Red Sox moved into Fenway Park in 1912, Lewis personally took ownership of left field, including that sloping incline of turf in front of the wall that thereafter became known as "Duffy's Cliff." "I'd go out to the ballpark mornings and have somebody hit the ball again and again to the wall," he said. "I experimented with every angle of approach up the cliff until I learned to play the slope correctly. Sometimes it would be tougher coming back down than going up. With runners on base, you had to come off the climb throwing."

Indeed, whatever the baseball situation, Lewis always seemed poised and prepared. But then, he was never one to make excuses for himself or his teammates. "Some of the present players think they've got it tougher because of [night-time] scheduling and the long road trips," he told a Boston reporter in 1970, "but don't forget we played all day ball, out in the hot sun, and we had to wear wet cabbage leaves in our caps [to keep cool]. The clubhouse and trains were furnaces and the hotels weren't much better."

Lewis needed no excuses in game 4 as his clutch RBI double to left in the sixth inning off opposing Philadelphia starter George "Dut" Chalmers (eight hits in eight innings) lifted Boston to a 2-1 Columbus Day win over the Phillies. Dick Hoblitzell, who raced home on the blast, had gotten on base with a single into center field with one out. "If Columbus had been there to see this California lad perform," wrote the *Boston Herald*'s R. E. McMillin of Lewis, "he would have written back to Isabella that he had seen Ty Cobb, and that Ty Cobb was all the papers cracked him up to be. Certainly he looked like Ty Cobb on wheels all through, same ball player from hoof to roof. No one could blame Christy for the mistake."

Boston had gotten to Chalmers for a run in the third when the Philadelphia infield couldn't handle a slow roller off the bat of Harry Hooper, which scored Jack Barry from third base. "Just stay in there long enough and keep believing, and you'll get your share of the breaks," concluded winning pitcher Ernie Shore. Shore, who fanned four and walked four in yet another complete game outing, was touched up for his only earned run in the eighth when Cravath tripled with two outs and Fred Luderus plated him with a single into center, his third hit of the game.

The Phillies had outhit the Sox 8–7, but this was of little consolation to the losers. "Behind three games to one, our hopes were all but shattered," Alexander later admitted. Conversely, Boston's spirits were understandably soaring high, especially after coming out on the winning end of three consecutive 2–1 ballgames. All that remained then was to close out the Series back in Philadelphia for game 5, a task Carrigan believed his ball club was more than capable of accomplishing. "[It] would be the hardest of hard breaks for us to miss out now," he maintained.

If anything, most of the "hard breaks" to follow came at the Phillies' expense. For example, just prior to the opening of game 5, Alexander, who was scheduled to start, experienced arm discomfort during warm-ups. Realizing he "wasn't right," the Philadelphia ace opted for sitting out the contest. "I never wanted to pitch a game so much in my life," he claimed afterward. "How I would have loved to beat Boston in that fifth game and put us back in the Series!"

With Alexander out of the way, the Red Sox lineup had no problem figuring out his replacement, game 2 loser Erskine Mayer, who, according to one caustic account, "had as much stuff as a Russian soldier has money." They knocked him out of the box after only two and one-third innings, rapping out six hits for two earned runs. Larry Gardner accounted for the first Boston tally after he tripled to center and scored on a base hit by Jack Barry with two outs in the top of the third.

Hooper added another an inning later when he homered into the temporary bleacher section in center field that Philadelphia owner Bill Baker had specially erected before the Series in hopes of cashing in on the team's cresting popularity. "The ball took the barrier on the first bound and in the farthest corner of the entire playing field," the *Boston Journal* reported. (Until rule changes in the 1920s, balls bouncing into the stands were counted as home runs.)

But the runs only served to knot the score two-all, as the Phillies had roughed up Boston starter Rube Foster (three earned runs on nine hits in nine innings) for a pair in the first. Fred Luderus, who ended up leading his team in RBIs during the Series with six, provided the key blow with a two-out, two-run double to left center.

The Phillies got to Foster again in the bottom of the fourth when Luderus homered over the right field wall and second baseman John Niehoff scored on a rare errant throw to third by Hooper. That gave the Phillies a 4–2 lead, but the margin was by no means enough to make any of the twenty thousand in attendance at Baker Bowl feel overly comfortable. For sure enough, the Sox came charging back in the eighth with Series standout Duffy Lewis leading the way. With teammate Del Gainor on first after reaching on an infield hit, Lewis deposited his third homer of the year into the left-field stands.

"I have witnessed all of the contests for the game's highest honors in the last 30 years and I want to say that the all-around work of the modest Californian never has been equaled in a big Series," gushed the *Globe*'s T. H. Murnane.

Lewis's timely blow had evened matters 4–4, but it was Hooper's second round-tripper of the game, a one-out blast to "that same infernal patch of temporary seats he sent the ball [earlier]," that won the game and the Series for Boston in the ninth. "What's so strange about that?" Shore mused years later. "Why, over the course of the whole season we hit only fourteen home runs. That's right, fourteen home runs for the whole season. Then we go into that last game and hit three. Hooper hit as many that day as he hit all year."

Regardless of how they won it, the Red Sox had become champions of the baseball world for the second time in four seasons, a considerable accomplishment that was not lost on their legions of fans or the journalists who covered them. "Perhaps there are yellow folks in some heavy-scented island on the Indian Ocean, or dusky kings in the wilds of Central Africa, or mad wild chieftains in Central [Tibet] that do not know that the Boston Red Sox are their champions," noted the writer R. E. McMillin in the kind of culturally insensitive prose that was all too common for the era. "But that [doesn't] alter the fact that the Sox own the earth and fullness thereof, and that their war clubs are the war clubs of the kings of their chosen pastime."

It also didn't alter the fact that despite winning eighteen games on the season, Babe Ruth had been denied by his manager an opportunity to pitch in the Series. "I ate my heart out on the bench in that Series," Ruth later complained. But with Shore and Foster turning in stellar performances on the mound, there was little need or desire on Carrigan's part to start the temperamental rookie. "Bill later told me," Ruth revealed, "if there had been a sixth game I surely would have pitched it, but we won the Series before any sixth game was necessary."

Fortunately for Ruth and the Sox, there would be no shortage of pitching opportunities for the former juvenile delinquent to distinguish himself in the postseasons to come.

CHAPTER FOUR
AFTER SPOKE (1916)

As 1915 gave way to 1916, the bloody stalemate in Europe continued. Despite suffering casualties numbering in the millions, neither the leaders of the Allies nor of the Central Powers saw fit to sue for peace. Instead they sought total victory on the battlefield, cease-fires and truces be damned. This rigid, uncompromising stance was not surprisingly at odds with the thinking of frontline soldiers on both sides. "One keeps cherishing the hope that it may be possible to find some way out of this miserable situation," wrote one dismayed German. "People both here and in other countries are crying out for the war to end, and yet it does not end. Who is responsible for this?"

The killing reached a grisly climax during the Battle of Verdun, an epic bloodletting which raged from February to December along the Meuse River in northeastern France. An estimated three hundred thousand French and German soldiers lost their lives during this engagement, which was dubbed the greatest battle of the war. A French company commander named Henri Desagneaux described the desperate scene: "There's death everywhere. At our feet, the wounded groan in a pool of blood, two of them, more seriously hit, are breathing their last. . . . Frightful, terrible moments, while the cannons harry us and we are splattered with mud and earth by the shells. For hours, these groans and supplications continue until, at 6 p.m., they die before our eyes without anyone being able to help them."

In America the war overseas became a major point of contention during the fall presidential campaign. Republicans, led by their standard-bearer, former New York governor and Supreme Court justice Charles Evans Hughes, charged that President Woodrow Wilson had been derelict in upholding the prestige and moral standing of a still neutral United States against the expansionist policies of the Kaiser and his minions. Only a full-scale buildup of America's armed forces and a more aggressive diplomatic posture could reverse this disturbing trend, they argued. Wilson, who would go on to narrowly win reelection, was having none of it. "Force, he said, "will not accomplish anything that is permanent . . . in the great struggle which is now going on the other side of the sea."

Red Sox baseball offered scant diversion from the unrelentingly depressing news from the front that spring. On April 9, team management announced it had traded Tris Speaker, arguably the most popular and accomplished performer in franchise history, to the Cleveland Indians for $55,000 and two unproven rookies. "No longer will Spoke do his feats of magic in centrefield for the Hub hose," lamented the *Boston Herald*. "No longer will he make good pitchers appear marvels by reason of his great catches." Speaker himself appeared taken aback by the deal. "I have never played ball with any other big league team than the Red Sox," he said. "Of course, I hate to go, but baseball is a business and you've got to be ready for anything and everything."

Just hours before the deal became official, Speaker clubbed a game-winning homer against the Dodgers during the team's final exhibition game of the spring at Ebbets Field, Brooklyn's handsome two-tiered ballpark that opened in the borough's former "Pigtown" area in 1913. In the joyous visitors' clubhouse afterward, Sox owner Joseph Lannin had gone out of his way to lavish praise on the star outfielder. "Great stuff, Spoke," Lannin said. But before Speaker had even checked out of his Brooklyn hotel room, he was

Speaker's trade to the Cleveland Indians on the eve of the 1916 season shocked Boston and the baseball world. "When a team loses such a tower of strength as Tris is," rival Detroit Tigers manager Hughie Jennings commented, "it is a certainty that the team is going to feel it." (Courtesy of the Boston Red Sox.)

approached by Cleveland general manager Rob McRoy with news of the trade. Speaker couldn't believe what he was hearing. "Why, that's crazy!" he exclaimed.

Speaker had good reason to be confused. Although he had been playing without a contract all spring, Lannin had personally assured him following the Brooklyn contest that he would remain with the Red Sox on the salary terms he sought, a reported $15,000 a year. "You win," Lannin reportedly said. Of course, he was lying.

The actual groundwork for Speaker's departure had been laid the previous December as the Federal League, the third major league, which had been giving AL and NL owners a severe case of economic jitters since 1914, called it quits. Too much red ink and an unsuccessful antitrust lawsuit against their more established league rivals proved to be the Federals' undoing. "With competition stifled," notes historian John P. Rossi, "major league owners began to reduce salaries to pre-Federal League levels." That included Speaker's. Lannin wanted "the great Texan" to accept a 50 percent pay cut. Speaker, who had made $18,000 in 1915, flatly refused, thus putting him at loggerheads with his boss.

Never one to take a business negotiation lying down, Lannin quietly began shopping Speaker around the league until he found a taker in Cleveland. According to Lannin, the Indians made "a most flattering offer," one he couldn't in good conscience refuse. "It was a big surprise to me," he claimed.

But Speaker was determined to have the last laugh. Before he decided to report to Cleveland, he demanded that Lannin fork over $5,000 of the purchase price that the Boston owner had received for his former charge. Lannin did not take kindly to this new development. "I will absolutely refuse to give one cent of the purchase price to Speaker or encourage him in his attitude," he thundered.

Speaker was equally uncompromising in his stance, declaring that he would just as soon retire from the game than come away empty handed. Fortuitously for both parties, Cleveland owner James C. Dunn stepped in with a generous two-year, $30,000 contract along with a $2,500 signing bonus to end the stalemate and get Speaker immediately into an Indians uniform. "I am a firm believer in 'You've got to spend money to make money,' and in this instance I figured that I would have to spend 'big money' if I hoped to cash in on my baseball investment," Dunn explained.

Word of the transaction hit Bostonians like an unwelcome spring snowstorm. "Tris Speaker's departure from the Red Sox is probably the greatest body blow ever dealt a Boston team," wrote Arthur Duffey of the *Boston Post*. "The departure of Cy Young . . . and other erstwhile stars, caused considerable commotion among the fans, but nothing in comparison to the talk of Speaker's passing.

. . . Here is a player at the height of his career. He never played better ball than the past season. The bulwark of defense in the outfield, he has been responsible for two world's championship pennants coming to the Hub. All that we can say is, 'Wait and see how the deal works out.'"

One angry fan was unwilling to demonstrate such patience. P. R. Warren of Brookline claimed to a reporter that the club had permanently alienated its most loyal supporters. "President Lannin has made the biggest mistake of his life in the sale of Speaker to Cleveland," he said. "Personally I go up to Fenway Park to see Speaker in action and I know there are many others like myself."

Baseball notables around the league were likewise dumbfounded by the move. Detroit Tigers manager Hughie Jennings believed the Sox had severely jeopardized their ability to repeat as league champions. Washington Senators owner Clark Griffith remarked that Boston was downright "foolish" to ship Speaker out of town. "He was in a class by himself," Griffith explained.

As for the team itself, the mood was downcast in the Sox clubhouse. Speaker certainly had his share of personal enemies in the locker room, especially among the Knights of Columbus faction, but everyone recognized his great ball-playing skills and overall value to the club. It appeared that winning had suddenly gotten a little harder for Boston. "Resignation to the inevitable is the spirit that characterizes the Boston team today," reported the *Boston Post*. "They have by no means lost all their spirit or their fight, but a world of confidence has departed from the ranks. The men feel that they have been tremendously handicapped at the very start and that unthinking Boston fans may show a disposition to criticise them for a mistake for which they had not the slightest responsibility and which was directly opposed to their own best interests."

To make matters worse, the team would be heading into the regular season without one of its top starting pitchers from the previous year. Smokey Joe Wood decided to sit out the upcoming baseball campaign on his Pennsylvania farm. "I retired," he later told

Smokey Joe Wood was another unexpected departure. Although he had fallen from his lofty 1912 pitching heights, he had still managed to record fourteen victories in 1915 in spite of crippling arm pain. (Courtesy of the Boston Red Sox.)

the writer Lawrence Ritter. "I . . . fed the chickens, and just thought and thought about the whole situation. Only twenty-six years old and all washed up. A has-been. I put up a trapeze in the attic, and I'd hang on that for hours to stretch my arm out. Maybe that would help—who could say? But it didn't."

Eventually Wood got it into his head to make a comeback, albeit not as the lights-out right-hander who had once effortlessly mowed down opposing batsmen. "So what if I couldn't pitch anymore?" he asked himself. With the Red Sox front office blessing, he managed to work out a deal for himself, landing in Cleveland for a $15,000 purchase price.

"Lee Fohl was managing Cleveland at the time, and he encouraged me every way he could," Wood said. "And for my part I tried to show him that I could do more than pitch. I played in the infield during fielding practice, I shagged flies in the outfield, I was ready to pinch-run, to pinch-hit—I'd have carried the water bucket if they had water boys in baseball. The hell with my pride. . . . I was just another ballplayer who wanted a job and wanted it bad."

Acknowledging that the departure of Speaker had dealt a serious blow to team morale, Bill Carrigan characteristically decided to confront the issue head on. Overhearing an early season clubhouse conversation between Babe Ruth and several other players lamenting their predicament, the feisty Boston manager gave the pep talk of his life. "All right, we lost Speaker," he tersely said. "But we're still a tight ball club. We got good pitching, good fielding, and we'll hit well enough. If you guys stop your moaning and get down to business we can win the pennant again."

Luckily for Carrigan, he had an unexpected ace up his sleeve. Just prior to dealing Speaker to Cleveland, Joseph Lannin sent $3,500 over to the St. Louis Browns for the services of temperamental outfielder Clarence "Tilly" Walker. Though it didn't seem like much of a deal at the time, Walker's arrival in a Red Sox uniform saved the club from having to scramble for a quality replacement for Speaker once the Cleveland deal went down. That's because Walker was a seasoned pro with considerable outfield experience and a strong throwing arm. He had even led the AL in assists with twenty-seven in 1915.

But it was with his bat that this one-time telegraph operator from Limestone, Tennessee, staked his big-league reputation. Over the previous five seasons, he had averaged over .280 while blasting a career-high sixteen triples in 1914. The one major knock against him, however, was that his frequent mood swings could get in the way of his performance on the field.

As one highly critical account put it, "He is said to be quite a hitter when he feels like hitting, but grouches and sulks when he does not whang a double or a triple every few minutes. In other words he worries more about his batting average than about the club's record of games won."

Although Walker's performance with the Red Sox did not cause many Boston fans to abandon their deep disappointment over the Speaker trade, he nonetheless did provide an acceptable stopgap measure in center field. For the season, he made 290 putouts and twelve assists in 128 games to go with a .266 batting average. Yet this all-around solid showing could not help Boston breeze to its third pennant in five years.

The problem lay in the batting lineup. The Sox could manage only a pitiable .248 team average while scoring the third lowest number of runs in the AL with 550. They weren't exactly hitless wonders, but they were a far cry from the Speaker-led 1912 club that bludgeoned its way to a league-leading 799 runs.

Fortunately for Hub fans, this edition of the Red Sox possessed an outstanding pitching corps to make up for the pathetic lack of offense. Indeed, Boston had no other junior-circuit competitor comparable to them in the arms department. On any given day, the team could deploy the heavy-duty likes of Babe Ruth, Dutch Leonard, Carl Mays, Ernie Shore, and Rube Foster against their opposition. As a group, they threw a league-leading twenty-four shutouts, including a pair of no-hitters by Foster and Leonard against the Yankees and Browns respectively.

But in Ruth, the club had an unsurpassed ace. He led the staff in wins (23), strikeouts (170), complete games (23), innings pitched (324), shutouts (9), winning percentage (.657), and earned runs allowed (1.75). In short, he was the best pitcher in baseball outside of Walter Johnson. And there he had a distinct advantage as he went 5–0 against the "Big Train" that season in head-to-head meetings.

Still, Ruth could be a handful. Since the previous season, Carrigan had made a special point of rooming with his troublesome yet endearing left-hander. The underlying idea here was that Ruth would never dare step out for a night on the town partying and

Boston management replaced Speaker with the temperamental Clarence "Tilly" Walker. According to one highly critical account, "He is said to be quite a hitter when he feels like hitting, but grouches and sulks when he does not whang a double or triple every few minutes." (Courtesy of the Library of Congress.)

drinking to all hours with his skipper so closely monitoring him. Guess again. "One night, I recall I turned my back just long enough to look in a mirror to put on a tie," Carrigan said. "When I turned around the Babe had disappeared."

On another evening that Ruth had managed to elude his watchful gaze, Carrigan received an urgent phone call from the police. Apparently his star pitcher had been arrested. The local authorities wanted Carrigan to come down to the station house and post bail. "I'll bail him out tomorrow morning," a weary Carrigan responded. "That way, I'll know where he'll be for tonight."

Like so many superstar athletes that would follow in his footsteps in the decades ahead, success and its fellow traveler fame had come too quickly and easily. For a wide-eyed kid fresh out of Catholic reform school with little formal education, Ruth simply had nothing to draw on from his own deeply troubled personal background to prepare him for the demands of being a bona fide national celebrity.

"His life fell into an easily predictable pattern—FUN, in capital letters," noted his second wife, Claire Hodgson Ruth, whom he married in 1929 after a long-running and characteristically tempestuous romantic affair. "Most fun of all was freedom. Then baseball. Then all the things money can buy for a guy who is young and has a lot of things he has wanted to buy for years and years. This was a robust man and he wanted all the things robust men should want. Only unfortunately, in excess."

Carrigan tried to curb this immoderate behavior by telling Ruth that his actions were hurting the team. "I asked him how he'd like it if I called a meeting of the players, stood him up and pointed to him as a player who was costing the Red Sox games by not behaving himself," Carrigan said.

When this approach failed with his unruly charge, Carrigan resorted to suspending Ruth's salary and putting him on a modest allowance of $10 a week. "The rest of his money we held and gave to him at the close of the season," Carrigan related. While an imperfect solution, this drastic action did produce results. "Babe's conduct, under the restrictions we imposed on him, improved steadily," Carrigan said. "He never became Lord Fauntleroy under me or under any other manager to the end of his long and brilliant career. But he was an outstanding pitcher for the Red Sox and the game's outstanding player for years and years as a Yankee homerun king."

For Ruth's part, he never held it against Carrigan that such severe disciplinary measures were necessary. In fact, he always voiced the utmost respect and warmth for his old boss. "He was the greatest manager I ever played for," Ruth said.

Even with Ruth dominating from the mound, the Red Sox were in for a dogfight of a pennant race. But unlike in 1915, when only Detroit provided strong opposition, Boston saw a rapidly improved Chicago White Sox join the Tigers as serious pennant contenders. For sure, there was much to like about dictatorial Chicago owner Charles Comiskey's outfit. They had plenty of speed, hitting, and defense. Former Cleveland Indian "Shoeless" Joe Jackson batted a team-best .341 with 202 hits, 293 total bases, and 78 RBIs.

His teammate Eddie Collins, who had been sold to Chicago from Philadelphia for $50,000 the previous year, stretched his streak of consecutive seasons batting over .300 to eight. He also led all AL second basemen with a .976 fielding average. Where the White Sox fell a little short was in pitching. While Eddie Cicotte, Claude "Lefty" Williams, and Urban "Red" Faber were all capable hurlers, averaging double figures in victories, they were still a year away from jelling as a staff.

Nonetheless, they and the Tigers gave the Red Sox all they could handle in 1916. In fact, the race itself was not decided until the next to last week of the season. With only percentage points separating them atop the AL standings, the Red Sox and Tigers squared off for a critical three-game series in Detroit on September 19–21. Boston took the first game when Carl Mays was able to pitch out of a pair of late-inning jams to produce a 3–1 victory. "He . . . extricated himself in masterly style," wrote John J. Hallahan in the *Boston Herald*.

The second contest was much closer, yet the end result remained the same. The Sox overcame an early 3–0 Tiger lead and escaped

In 1916, Ruth was arguably the best pitcher in baseball outside of Walter Johnson, with twenty-three wins and a 1.75 ERA. "Everyone talks about my hitting; how about my pitching?" the future "Sultan of Swat" later complained. (Courtesy of the Boston Red Sox.)

with a 4–3 win. Olaf Henriksen's RBI single to right field in the eighth was the deciding blow. "I pointed out to my gang [before the series started] that the time had come for them to put up or shut up," Carrigan later explained.

In the rubber game, Babe Ruth received the starting nod and offered up a gem, tossing a seven-hitter and going the distance in a 10–2 Boston rout. The Tigers "were like toys in his hands," Hallahan wrote. Ruth was especially effective in the seventh inning when he struck out Detroit hit leaders Ty Cobb and Bobby Veach on six consecutive pitches. "It was a great performance and the like of it had never been witnessed before in Frank Navin's Park," the *Boston Globe* declared. The Sox offense, meanwhile, did its part, piling up thirteen hits, four of them for extra bases.

"Sure, I was worried at times, but I never gave a thought to the possibility that we might be beaten out," Carrigan said. The series sweep pushed the Tigers a full three games behind Boston with just a handful of contests left to play, thus all but ending their pennant hopes and giving the Red Sox their second straight AL championship. As for the White Sox, they faded in the closing weeks, although they managed to edge out Detroit for second place overall in the final standings.

As always, Larry Gardner had a major part in bringing about a winning Boston outcome, playing arguably the best ball of his career. He hit a team-best .308 on the season and continued to be a pillar of the club's infield defense at third, making 149 putouts and 278 assists. In recognition of this stellar glovework, he was known around the league as "the Diving Third Baseman."

The son of a small-town grocer, Gardner filled his youthful days in Enosburg Falls, Vermont, fishing and playing whatever sport was in season. While he displayed a special talent for ice hockey (he was captain of his high school squad), he made an even bigger impression on the baseball diamond. He hit .432 his senior year and surrendered only eight runs in as many starts as a pitcher. "Why, I was just like any other small boy and baseball was my one big thought," he later said. "Always playing ball I was—morning, noon, night and on all other occasions."

After graduation, he enrolled at the University of Vermont, where he majored in chemistry and resumed his boyhood obsession with the national pastime. Though he dropped to a .269 average in his first year of intercollegiate competition, this "child marvel from Enosburg Falls" did not become overly discouraged. He instead demonstrated a buoyant resiliency by earning UVM team captain honors and batting .400 as a sophomore for the Catamounts. As one student publication noted, "He was strong at the bat and wonderful at base running, his fielding was well nigh errorless, while his throwing was swift and sure as fate."

Such developed skills, coming as they did from a local product, did not long escape the notice of the Red Sox. While playing in the

Third baseman Larry Gardner was a fun-loving and easygoing New Englander, whom one writer once described as having "a disposition as sweet as the wildflowers that grow on the mountains of Vermont," was just happy being a big leaguer. (Courtesy of the Boston Red Sox.)

Maine State League during the summer of 1908, Gardner was paid a fateful visit by a Boston scout. "He signed me on the spot for four hundred dollars a month, just during the season," Gardner recalled over a half-century later. "I left the Maine league with them promising to send me the eighty-five dollars they owed me. The mails must be real slow; I haven't received it yet."

While the mails might have been slow, Gardner's ascent to big-league stardom was not. He appeared in 113 games as a fill-in second baseman with the parent club in 1910 and made the permanent move over to third the following season. He immediately commanded people's attention, hitting .283 and handling the hot corner with all the effortless grace and aplomb of a grizzled veteran. "Larry could play third base with the best of them," praised Smokey Joe Wood. "I wouldn't trade him for five Frank Bakers."

Opponents like Ty Cobb were reluctantly inclined to agree. Universally regarded as the best bunter in baseball, the combative Detroit outfielder could not purchase a hit against Gardner. "I found out Ty's secret early and never told him," Gardner confessed to the writer Henry Berry. "You see, Ty used to fake a lot of bunts. But when he was going to really bunt, he'd always lock his lips. When I saw that, I'd start in with the pitch. He never realized I caught on."

Apart from depriving the Deadball Era's most famous batsman of hits, Gardner also held the unique distinction of being a roommate of Babe Ruth when the team traveled, which is to say he never enjoyed the pleasure of the Babe's company. "He never unpacked his bags," Gardner later told a friend. "He never stays with me in the room when I'm on the road. He's always living with women." Gardner added that one of his earliest memories of Ruth involved the future slugger being serviced by a prostitute while lying on the floor "smoking a cigar and eating peanuts."

Although Gardner seems to have stayed away from brothels and the temptations they provided (he was a happily married man), he did enjoy a night on the town now and then and hoisting a few alcoholic beverages, like so many of his contemporaries. Among the

For the second year in a row, Ty Cobb and his Detroit Tiger teammates battled the Red Sox for the league title. (Courtesy of the Library of Congress.)

drinking partners he could count in his wide circle of baseball friends was all-time pitching great Cy Young, who pitched his last year in a Boston uniform when Gardner was a rookie in 1908. Young went out of his way to prop up Gardner's confidence when the self-described "green country boy" had a particularly brutal defensive day at third in a game against the New York Highlanders.

"We went over to the Hotel Putnam on Huntington Avenue," Gardner recalled almost seventy years later. "That's where most of the players used to go in those days. Cy ordered some rye whiskey called Cascade—how he loved that Cascade. Don't see it anymore. Then he told me not to worry, everyone's nervous at first; I'd be all right. Well, that sure picked me up. Imagine drinking whiskey with Cy Young and being told you were going to make it! He was quite a guy!"

Until he was traded away to the Athletics after the 1917 season, Gardner was a reliable mainstay of the Red Sox offense, averaging .282, fifteen doubles, and thirteen steals a season. But his real value came in the late innings of tight contests when he could be invariably counted on to produce the big defensive stop or timely hit. Gardner "was the best clutch hitter in the league," notes baseball historian Mike Sowell. A case in point was his game-wining sacrifice fly in the deciding contest of the 1912 World Series.

"When I first hit it, I thought it was going out," he later remembered. "Then I saw [New York Giants outfielder] Josh Devore catch it near the fence and I was disappointed for a second. But then I saw [the winning run score] and I realized it was over. It meant four thousand twenty-four dollars and sixty-eight cents to me [in winning Series share money] which just about doubled my earnings that year." A truer money player, there never was.

For Bill Carrigan, the 1916 flag easily represented the sweetest moment of his managerial career. His team had overcome long odds, including internal club strife and a draining pennant fight, to become the undisputed masters of the AL. When "the pressure was really on them, they could arise to the occasion better than any club I ever saw," he later boasted. Nonetheless, there was still a World

Series to be played. And presenting a major obstacle to Boston's chances of repeating as champs were the dangerous Brooklyn Dodgers, victors of the NL and winners of ninety-four games.

The Dodgers were managed by the eccentric Wilbert Robinson, a rotund Hudson, Massachusetts, native. And the team had survived a grueling pennant race to rival Boston's. Battling the Phillies, Braves, and Giants for the NL lead most of the summer, Robinson's club got hot down the stretch to capture the title by two and one-half games. Predictably, Giants manager John McGraw, an acerbic man who openly scorned the notion of good sportsmanship, was not gracious in defeat. He made the baseless accusation that his team had quit against Brooklyn during a crucial late September game at the Polo Grounds that clinched the pennant for the visitors. The usually jovial Robinson, a former close friend and teammate of McGraw's, took great offense at these charges. "That's a lot of shit," he exclaimed.

McGraw's sour grapes notwithstanding, there was no reason to question the legitimacy of Brooklyn's accomplishment. Bedecked in their distinctive checkered uniforms, the Dodgers had led the NL in hitting with a .261 team average and in pitching with a 2.12 staff ERA. Not for nothing then were such esteemed baseball figures as Grover Cleveland Alexander predicting a competitive Series. "I have pitched to both teams and have seen quite a lot of the Dodgers," Alexander wrote in a guest column for the *Boston Post*, "and anyone who thinks the Red Sox are going to have a picnic is going to be badly fooled." To be sure, Brooklyn possessed several strengths, starting with its explosive batting order.

Paced by the .300 hitting of left fielder Zack Wheat and first baseman Jake Daubert, the Dodgers were able to score the second most runs in the NL with 585. The owner of a lifetime .317 batting average with 1,261 RBIs, Wheat has been frequently cited as "the best player" to wear Dodger blue prior to the coming of Jackie Robinson and his "Boys of Summer" teammates in the late 1940s.

"I think I will hit all right up here," Wheat said after breaking in as a regular with the club in 1909. If anything, he was underestimat-

The eccentric manager of the National League champion Brooklyn Dodgers, Wilbert Robinson, once attempted (unsuccessfully) to catch a grapefruit dropped from a passing biplane. (Courtesy of the Library of Congress.)

ing his ability as an offensive force. A left-handed hitter with considerable line-drive power, the no-nonsense Wheat, a half-Cherokee from Missouri, flourished within the cozy confines of Ebbets Field, his home ballpark for fifteen of his nineteen seasons in the majors. Indeed, he hit .300 or better twelve times during that period. His performance throughout the 1916 campaign was likewise exemplary.

He compiled a .316 average to go with 177 hits, 32 doubles, 13 triples, and 9 home runs. "He was a man who simply took care of business," notes baseball historian and statistician Bill James.

Daubert was no less committed in his approach to the game. Though he lacked the raw power numbers of Wheat, the stylish Pennsylvanian could hit for high average, winning consecutive NL batting titles in 1913 and 1914 with .350 and .329 marks. He also was a skilled bunter, making use of his superior foot speed to get on base.

"He uster put a reverse on it like a pool ball. It would hit the ground and—oops—here it is coming back," recalled teammate Casey Stengel, the future Hall of Fame manager who hit a respectable .279 as Robinson's starting center fielder in 1916. Nor was Daubert a slouch with the glove. In an era that was dominated by such slick fielding first basemen as Hal Chase of the New York Yankees, Daubert more than held his own at the bag. In fact, he was a standout, leading the league in fielding percentage three times during the span of his fifteen-year big-league career.

On the mound, the Dodgers relied on the veteran arms of Jeff Pfeffer and Rube Marquard. The younger brother of former big-league pitcher Frank Pfeffer, who had compiled an unremarkable 31–40 record in six seasons with the Braves and Cubs, Pfeffer was a hard throwing right-hander that Brooklyn had stolen from the perennially mismanaged St. Louis Browns organization. A twenty-three-game winner in 1914, Pfeffer had an even better season during Brooklyn's drive for the pennant, garnering a career-high twenty-five victories with an outstanding 1.92 ERA in 328 innings. In total, he would win 113 games during his Dodger tenure, in addition to helping the club to another league title in 1920. "This fellow Pfeffer is quite a pitcher," wrote syndicated sports columnist Hugh S. Fullerton.

The same was once said of Marquard during his heyday with the Giants. But after suffering through a twenty-two-loss campaign in 1914, he was coldly dumped by Giants skipper John McGraw. Determined to prove that McGraw had made a mistake, Marquard embraced the opportunity of resurrecting his flagging career when

Robinson picked him up on waivers the following summer. "Robbie was always looking to put something over on McGraw," the southpaw later revealed. While he could manage but two measly victories for Brooklyn that season, Marquard came back strong in 1916, notching thirteen wins and holding opposing teams to under two runs a game. "So everything worked out pretty well," he said.

In spite of the formidable talent arrayed against his ball club, Bill Carrigan professed not to be overly concerned about his team's chances in the upcoming Fall Classic. "We are ready for the battle to begin," the Boston manager averred, "and we hope to annex another championship. My men are full of confidence."

Most baseball experts could not find fault with this attitude. As moonlighting Detroit star Ty Cobb wrote in a column for the *Boston Post*, "To my mind the thing sizes up about this way: The Red Sox should win, for they have the pitchers to hold the Brooklyn sluggers and the few runs they will make [due to Brooklyn's own standout pitching] will be sufficient."

Ironically, runs were not at a premium for either team in game 1 as Boston outlasted the Dodgers 6–5 before an unusually subdued crowd of thirty-six thousand at Braves Field on October 7. As in the previous year's Series, Sox owner Joseph Lannin again opted to go with the higher seating capacity of his cross-town rivals' home ballpark over Fenway Park.

"I never saw a baseball crowd with less enthusiasm," the *Boston Globe*'s T. H. Murnane observed. "The followers of the Red Sox felt sure of their champions, while friends of the Brooklyn club were a bit shy in confidence. The Brooklyn players failed to show any gayety outside that displayed by Wilbert Robinson, evidently for the effect it would have on his men."

Indeed, the Dodgers had little to feel good about through the first eight innings. The Sox broke out to a 6–1 lead and starter Ernie Shore held Brooklyn bats in check, allowing just one run in the top of the fourth inning when Zack Wheat tripled home Casey Stengel with one out. The Dodgers might have scored more in the frame had Harry

Hooper not made a spectacular double play off a hard-hit ball to right field by George Cutshaw, the Brooklyn second baseman.

"There did not seem to be a chance in the world for Hooper to get near the ball," opined Paul Shannon of the *Boston Post*, "yet by a wonderful piece of sprinting he finally got under it, held on, but slipped and fell as a result of his sudden stoppage of speed." Expecting the ball to drop in for extra bases, Wheat had to hastily retreat back to third to tag up before resuming his trek home. "But Hooper," Shannon wrote, "jumping to his feet, made one of his beautiful and accurate pegs, the ball just beating the runner to the plate."

The Dodgers didn't generate any more noise until the ninth, when a tiring Shore lost his fastball and loaded the bases with one out. Just the same, after going up two strikes on next batter Mike Mowrey, Shore appeared poised to get out of the jam by inducing the weak-hitting Brooklyn infielder to hit an easy grounder to the normally dependable Hal Janvrin at second.

But Janvrin, who was filling in for injured starter Jake Barry, couldn't get a handle on the play, allowing the ball to skip by him into the outfield. Two runs scored, dropping the Sox lead to 6–3. Brooklyn added another when Ivy Olson scratched out an infield single and Shore issued a two-out, bases-loaded walk to pinch-hitter Fred Merkle, an old Boston foe from the 1912 World Series.

"Are you gasping now?" the *New York Times* asked its readers in a running game commentary afterward. "Well, many thousands at Braves Field were gasping at this juncture, although the propriety of gasping in public is a debated question in Boston." His hand thus forced, Carrigan made the inevitable pitching change, going with the side-winding right-hander Carl Mays, an eighteen-game winner on the regular season.

And though he was immediately greeted with an RBI single by Hy Myers to bring the Dodgers to within one run of the lead, Mays maintained his composure. He induced Jake Daubert to ground out, thereby extinguishing the Brooklyn rally and securing the first and only World Series save of his career. "The fact was," wrote T. H.

Murnane, "that up to the ninth the Boston club looked like all class, while the men from the south side of the big bridge looked like shadow champions. As it was, the Boston men seemed much stronger than Brooklyn as a ball team."

The Red Sox were able to give off that impression, courtesy of their suddenly hot offense. Deservedly dismissed for most of the season as a weak-hitting outfit, Boston banged out five extra base hits in the contest, all of them coming against losing Brooklyn pitcher Rube Marquard (seven hits, four walks, in seven innings pitched). Specially selected by Robinson to start over regular season stopper Jeff Pfeffer to counter the predominantly left-handed hitting Sox lineup, Marquard turned out to be something of a bust. After holding Boston scoreless through the first two innings, the veteran portsider gave up single runs in the third and sixth innings off RBI hits by Duffy Lewis and Tilly Walker.

But the real damage came in the seventh when Boston erupted for three runs. Hal Janvrin led off with a double to right and came round to score when Dodger middle infielders Ivy Olson and George Cutshaw suddenly found themselves incapable of handling a pair of routine balls hit by Walker and Dick Hoblitzell. "The Brooklyn infield cracked wide open," noted the *Boston Herald*'s John J. Hallahan.

That crack only seemed to widen when a subsequent late throw to the plate by Cutshaw and a sacrifice fly by Everett Scott permitted Walker and Hoblitzell to register Boston's fourth and fifth tallies of the game. Although it didn't seem important at the time, Boston added an insurance run in the bottom of the eighth. Janvrin doubled home Hooper after the latter had been issued a one-out walk by Pfeffer, who had come on in relief for Marquard.

In spite of Boston's rejuvenated hitting attack, the main topic of conversation after the game was Hooper's shoestring catch in the seventh. "That was the turning point of the game," lamented Brooklyn pitcher Jack Coombs, the former Philadelphia Athletics star who had notched thirteen wins for the Dodgers that season.

"Our offensive was snapped at a point when it was apparent to all that we were on the road to making several runs."

Coming up big in pressure situations had always been a distinctive quality of Hooper. The shy and unassuming son of a California rancher, Hooper had an upbringing straight out of the pages of a Mark Twain novel. "What a boyhood!" he later exclaimed. "I rode horseback to and from school, six miles each way. I had a rifle and a shotgun, and there was a great plenty . . . of deer, pheasant, ducks, geese, and quail [to hunt]." When he wasn't out tracking game, he could be found on a baseball diamond. "I played at every opportunity," he said. "Just holding a bat, or following the flight of a ball, gave me a greater thrill than holding a shotgun and watching the flight of a game bird."

Putting these finely honed skills to use, Hooper enrolled at St. Mary's College, a small Catholic school in Oakland that boasted an excellent baseball program. Baseball, however, was not the future Hall of Famer's sole reason for attending. "I expected to be an engineer," he later told Lawrence Ritter. Indeed, he graduated with a degree in civil engineering in 1907 and had every intention of pursuing that avocation until fate came knocking in the person of Red Sox owner John I. Taylor.

Seeking to bolster the talent level of his big-league roster, Taylor used all his Yankee charm and cunning to get Hooper's name on a Boston contract. It wasn't easy. Hooper, who hit .371 as a senior, had his mind set on becoming a civil engineer. Taylor turned this exhibited single-mindedness to his own advantage.

"It just so happens that we are thinking of building a new ball park in the not so distant future," Taylor slyly told him, "and we may be looking for someone just like you." Hooper took the bait. He signed with the Red Sox for $2,800, and although he never got around to using his engineering skills to build what would become Fenway Park, he didn't seem to mind. "I was out in right field there the whole time, drawing a line on a baseball instead of a chart," he said.

Hooper, who batted .281 and amassed an incredible 324 assists as an outfielder in seventeen major league seasons, was never one to brag about his accomplishments. His nickname, in fact, was "Modest Harry." Still, his standout talent was hard to miss, especially among his peers. "I remember a game against Detroit," Larry Gardner said. "There was a runner on third. Someone—I think it was Donie Bush—hit a short fly to right. Harry came tearing in and dove on his belly for the ball. He caught it, rolled over, and came up throwing. I'll be damned if he didn't get the runner at the plate. I never saw anything else like it." Tris Speaker was equally effusive. Hooper "actually threw strikes from the outfield," he claimed.

Most times, of course, Hooper didn't need to reveal his cannon arm at all, given his superb ability to chase down fly balls. New York Giant second baseman Larry Doyle found this out firsthand during the climactic game of the 1912 World Series. In the fifth inning, he hit a screaming line drive toward the bleachers in right center that seemed ticketed to leave the ballpark. Hooper had other ideas.

As he later recounted, "I took off for the fence when the ball was hit, turned, saw it coming over my shoulder and stuck out my bare hand. I caught it, but the fence was there and I was running into it. It was a low fence, so I jumped over and the crowd opened up. I can still see that instant as though everything was standing still, like a movie that is stopped. I can still see the ball right there."

A devout Catholic, Hooper once speculated that a higher power might have been responsible for his spectacular catch. At the outset of the contest, he had come upon a scrap of paper on the playing field with the image of the "Sacred Heart of Jesus" on it, along with an accompanying prayer. After reading the prayer and offering a private prayer of his own for team victory, he pocketed the paper and thought nothing of it until his clutch grab against Larry Doyle in the fifth. "[I] was in the exact spot and position to catch it and how I caught it was as if someone had placed it in my hand," he told historian Ellery H. Clark. "Then I jumped the [temporary] fence without crashing into someone who could have been badly hurt. Never lost my feet. All this has made me wonder ever since."

With Speaker's abrupt departure to Cleveland in the spring of 1916, Hooper's importance to the team became even more pronounced. Unspoken pressure was placed upon his broad shoulders to produce more at bat and in the field if the Red Sox were to have a realistic chance of repeating as league champions. He also added another chapter to his book of masterly outfield plays with 266 putouts, the second most of his career. "Boy, if there was any one characteristic of Harry Hooper's, it was that he was a clutch player," Smokey Joe Wood said.

Neither the Red Sox nor the Dodgers could be accused of playing like wildfire in game 2 as both teams hunkered down for a low-scoring fourteen-inning affair that was ultimately won by Boston, 2–1. Babe Ruth became the focal point of attention here, for despite being touched up for an inside-the-park home run by Brooklyn

In Speaker's absence, Hall of Fame outfielder Harry Hooper, pictured here beating the throw to third, carried the team offensively in 1916 with a club leading 156 hits, 75 runs scored, 80 walks, and 27 stolen bases. "When the chips were down that guy played like wildfire," Smokey Joe Wood once praised. (Courtesy of the Boston Public Library Print Department, Sports Temples of Boston Collection.)

center fielder Hy Myers in the top of the first inning, the big left-hander was practically flawless the rest of the way.

He blanked the Dodgers over the next thirteen innings, striking out four and scattering six hits in his first career World Series start. He also had a major hand in tying the game in the third. "They were playing Everett Scott close, and he pushed a line drive between Wheat and Myers [in left and center field respectively] and pulled up at third base for a triple," he recounted. "I then grounded to George Cutshaw at second base and Scottie crossed the plate with the tying run."

But Ruth wasn't ensured of the victory until Del Gainor, pinch-hitting for Larry Gardner, drove in teammate Mike McNally for the winning score in the bottom of the fourteenth inning. The .254-hitting McNally, a backup infielder by trade, had made this possible by drilling a single to left field off losing Brooklyn starter Sherrod Smith (seven hits, two strikeouts, in thirteen and one-third innings pitched). Smith, an experienced left-hander with a 14–10 regular season mark, had been a surprise pitching choice for Robinson, as the unpredictable Brooklyn manager once again chose to go with a southpaw against the Red Sox.

Said *Baseball Magazine*, "It would have been good policy either to have passed Gainor and trusted to Smith to get good results out of the bottom of the Boston batting list, or to have taken out the tiring Smith and sent in a fast right-hander to whiz them over the dark. But [Wilbert Robinson] made no change, and Gainor promptly smashed a left-field hit that scored McNally, and ended the discussion."

None of these curious managerial moves mattered one iota to Grantland Rice. According to the celebrated New York sports columnist, the game's outcome had nothing to do with personnel decisions made in the dugout and everything to do with karma. "Force of habit still stands as one of the controlling elements in the eternal Drive of Destiny," he wrote. "It gathers power as it moves along the narrow, winding highway of Fate. Boston formed the World Series habit 13 years ago today and she is surging along to her [fourth] post-season triumph with the bulk of Brooklyn's barrier blown from the right of way."

Convoluted automobile metaphors aside, Ruth was beside himself in feelings of personal vindication. "I know it was one of the happiest moments of my life," he later wrote of the win. "I had been waiting for two years to pitch against the National League champions, and I think I convinced Carrigan that I could hold them as well as any other pitcher on his staff." To emphasize this point, Ruth had buttonholed his manager for a private conversation in the Fenway clubhouse after the game. "I told you a year ago I could take care of those National League bums for you," he cheekily informed Carrigan, "but you never gave me a chance."

Suddenly trailing 2–0 in games and staring at the possibility of being on the wrong end of a World Series sweep, the "silent and flabby" Dodgers were admittedly not in the best of spirits when they departed from Fenway. Having been let down by their vaunted offense (club batting leaders Jake Daubert and Zack Wheat went a combined zero for ten in the contest), Brooklyn was now seemingly on its last legs and in desperate need of a morale boost. They got one the next day as timely hitting and some outstanding late-inning relief work by Jeff Pfeffer allowed the Dodgers to walk away with a 4–3 victory in game 3 at Ebbets Field.

"Brooklyn is ablaze with enthusiasm tonight," wrote the *Post*'s Paul Shannon. "Bonfires gleam on the scarred hills that surround [owner] Charlie Ebbets' ball park, and through the normally deserted streets of Brooklyn crowds of leather-lunged rooters are sounding the praises of Wilbert Robinson's men."

The Dodgers earned these expressions of gratitude by taking command of the game early. They scored single runs off Boston starter Carl Mays in the third and fourth innings on RBI singles by Cutshaw and starting pitcher Jack Coombs. Two more Brooklyn tallies followed in the fifth when Ivy Olson tripled into left center to drive in Wheat and infielder Mike Mowrey to make it 4–0.

Then things got interesting, but not in a necessarily good way for the Dodgers. Coombs, who had coasted through the first five innings, got roughed up in the sixth. After issuing a one-out walk to Olaf Henriksen, the Philly expatriate surrendered a triple to Hooper, scoring Boston's first run. The Sox picked up another one-out later when reserve outfielder Chick Shorten, a .295 hitter on the year, singled home Hooper. Although Coombs recovered to retire next batter Dick Hoblitzell for the inning's final out, neither he nor the Dodgers were out of danger.

Larry Gardner made sure of that the following inning when he hit a one-out, solo homer to right field that prompted Brooklyn outfielder Casey Stengel to angrily shake his arm "in disgust." "I hadn't been hitting and I was really mad," recalled Gardner, who hit .176 overall in the Series. "[Coombs] broke off a curve on me, a lefty hitter. I started to swing and tried to stop because I thought it was a bad pitch, but I was committed too far and had to go through with it. I even had my eyes shut. When I opened them, I saw the ball going over the wall. Can you believe that—hitting a home run with your eyes closed?"

The homer made it a one-run game, forcing Robinson to go to his bullpen. He brought in the heretofore underutilized Pfeffer, who had appeared briefly in game 1. Whether it was the frustration of being passed over to start by Robinson or an old-fashioned adrenaline rush, the six-foot, three-inch, 210-pound right-hander responded in true ace form. He struck out three and didn't allow a Boston player to reach base for the remainder of the contest. Brooklyn's first ever World Series victory was thus assured.

"There was none of the nervousness that marked the happier conflicts back in Boston," noted N. J. Flatley in the *Boston Herald*. "[The Dodgers] were fast and sure in the field, confident and effective at the bat. They were home to show their own loyal fans that they were worthy of a place in baseball's greatest struggle and they showed them."

Alas, this sense of euphoria did not last. Dutch Leonard took the hill for game 4, and after experiencing a rough first inning, he regained his bearings, limiting the Dodgers to five hits and one earned run in a complete game, 6–2 Boston win. "Well, it's all over now," taunted a Beantown supporter to the visibly dejected Brooklyn fans sitting around him in the Ebbets Field grandstand afterward. "Yes, all over now. . . . Yes, you can kiss this World Series goodbye right here and now."

It is unlikely that any such defeatist thoughts had entered the minds of the Dodgers when they teed off against Leonard in the opening frame. Lead-off man Jimmy Johnston, a lifetime .294 hitter, opened with a triple to right center on the first pitch. Hy Myers followed with a "clean single" up the middle that drove in Johnston for the first run of the game. Clearly upset by this early shellacking, the usually cool and collected Leonard proceeded to walk Fred Merkle. But the World Series veteran was cut down at second when Zack Wheat hit a fielder's choice grounder.

With Myers now on third with one out, George Cutshaw hit an infield grounder, this one getting past Sox second baseman Hal Janvrin for an error. Myers came home on the play and all of a sudden it seemed possible to the twenty-one thousand Flatbush faithful in attendance that Boston was going to lose its second straight Series contest.

Then the momentum shifted. Wheat was erased at third on a botched double steal attempt and Leonard punched out Mike Mowrey on strikes to end the inning. While two runs had scored, Leonard had managed to hang tough and survive. Things went downhill from there for the Dodgers as they could muster only three more hits against the crafty Ohioan. Observed the *New York Times*, "[After] giving the hopes of local fandom the pleasant thrills of a rapid ascent to the mountain peak, [Leonard] cast them from the summit and they were dashed to bits on the cruel rocks below."

Brooklyn's Rube Marquard, making his second Series start on three days' rest, didn't aid his team's cause by getting lit up for four earned runs on five hits in only four innings of work. Larry Gardner provided the key blow in the top of the second, smoking a 3–0 Marquard fastball into the outer reaches of center field for a three-run homer, his second of the Series.

Decades later, Casey Stengel would remind Gardner of his crowning moment of World Series glory upon a chance meeting with him in Boston during the 1940s. "I hadn't seen Casey in years," Gardner recalled. "He took one look at me and said, 'There's that third baseman that made me show my ass to the crowd chasing those home runs.'"

Boston followed up Gardner's homer with a pair of insurance runs in the fourth and fifth innings on RBI singles by Carrigan and Hooper. But the game's outcome had by that point become a moot point. "That one blow [by Gardner] . . . broke Marquard's heart, shattered Brooklyn's wavering defense, and practically closed out the series," opined Grantland Rice.

As if to give credence to Rice's analysis, the Dodgers weakly succumbed to the Red Sox the next day, losing game 5 and the championship by a score of 4–1 before an ecstatic crowd of forty-two thousand at Braves Field. "The nice thing about that last game was we won it right at home," winning pitcher Ernie Shore later told Donald Honig. "Our fans let go a really good shout for us when it was over. We got a standing ovation. It was the third world championship the team had given them in five years and they showed they appreciated it."

The crowd especially appreciated Shore's sterling performance. Chalking up his second victory of the Series, Shore fanned four and allowed but one walk and three hits in nine innings. "Shore had every man's number and was a complete master of the situation always," an impressed Ty Cobb wrote in the *Boston Post*. "He was very effective with his fast ball, using an occasional curve just to show the [Dodgers] what he had. There were very few hard hit balls off Ernie and the superiority of the Red Sox was very marked."

Shore's outing did not go entirely without a hitch, however. In the top of the second, Brooklyn's George Cutshaw, whom Shore had walked on four straight pitches to start the inning, scored from third on a passed ball. "I still remember that pitch," Shore recalled six decades later. "It broke so much it missed [Boston catcher Hick Cady's] mitt entirely. That's what my fastball would do. It sank awfully sharp and sometimes the catcher couldn't handle it."

The miscue made no difference. Shore's teammates cuffed around Brooklyn ace Jeff Pfeffer, who was at last getting his chance to start in the Series, for four runs in seven innings to put the game away. Boston got things rolling in the second. Following a one-out triple by Duffy Lewis, Larry Gardner hit a sacrifice fly to Wheat in left, driving in Lewis for his Series-leading sixth RBI of the postseason. Wheat "tried, but he never had a chance of [throwing out] Duff at the cashing in place," the *Boston Globe* reported.

The Sox added two more runs in the third on an RBI single by Chick Shorten and yet another costly misplay by Brooklyn's Ivy Olson at short, his fourth of the Series, that allowed Cady to score from second. "Ivy had a horrible Series and we didn't do anything to help him," Babe Ruth recalled. "We used to yell out, 'When in doubt hit to Ivy.' We had him crazy before it was over." Boston concluded its mini-scoring spree an inning later when Hal Janvrin doubled home Hooper for the final run.

"After losing the fourth and decisive contest to the Boston Red Sox, I guess even [Wilbert] Robinson himself and his men will admit that the Brooklyn club was outplayed at every stage," crowed Sox second baseman Jack Barry, who had been sidelined for the entire postseason due to a leg injury. "Results speak, and even the National League sympathizers who were hoping against hope must have become convinced after this closing contest that there was considerable difference in the class between the two clubs."

Indeed, Series statistics reveal that the Red Sox dominated play in every meaningful category. They outhit Brooklyn .238 to .200 while outscoring their NL counterparts by a nearly two to one margin. On the mound, the Sox were even more impressive. They posted a phenomenal 1.76 team ERA as opposed to a good but not great 3.04 showing for the Dodgers.

"We didn't think it was possible for anybody to beat us," Ernie Shore said.

He was correct.

CHAPTER FIVE
SPOILS OF WAR (1917–1918)

The once unthinkable became a reality by the early spring of 1917. After three years of maintaining a stringent if uneasy neutrality, the United States declared war on Germany, thereby entering the First World War on the side of Great Britain, France, and Russia. "The world must be made safe for democracy," proclaimed President Woodrow Wilson in his famed April 2 war message to Congress. "Its peace must be planted upon the tested foundations of political liberty."

America's road to war had begun with Germany's provocative decision to wage unrestricted submarine warfare in the frigid waters of the North Atlantic in late January. This meant that henceforward all neutral merchant vessels, including unarmed American ones, were fair game to marauding German U-boats. If this wasn't bad enough, word had also leaked out via an intercepted German diplomatic cable that the Kaiser's government was clandestinely seeking the aid of Mexico in launching a surprise military attack on the United States. Wilson, who had campaigned for reelection in 1916 as the man who "kept us out of war," had seen enough. "Our motive will not be revenge or the victorious assertion of the physical might of the nation, but only the vindication of right, of human right, of which we are only a single champion," he pledged.

Inspired by this lofty rhetoric, the country enthusiastically rallied behind the war effort. Tens of thousands of young men flocked to army and navy recruitment centers to voluntarily sign up for the fight. Those who didn't were required to register for a compulsory military draft, the first since the Civil War. "Greetings from the President," opened the official government letter notifying draftees of their impending duty. "You have been selected by a committee of your neighbors for service in your country's armed forces." Approximately five million American "citizen-soldiers" served in uniform during the conflict, including 227 big leaguers.

"This is a war of democracy against bureaucracy," announced NL president John K. Tener. "And I tell you that baseball is the very watchword for democracy." To demonstrate their commitment to the cause, in addition to generating favorable publicity for their franchises, team owners made a public show of marching their players in close-ordered military drill before games. But aside from such overt displays of patriotism, the war left no major imprint on the game during the first year of hostilities. "Baseball got through the 1917 season relatively undisturbed," notes historian John P. Rossi.

Rossi's observation, however, did not really describe the Red Sox. At the conclusion of the previous fall's World Series, Bill Carrigan stunned players and fans alike by following through on a late-season pledge to step down as Boston manager and retire to Maine.

"I had become a partner with a Lewiston man in ownership of a chain of movie theaters throughout New England," he later explained. "Most of my baseball savings of ten years was invested in this venture and I felt it deserved my undivided attention." Carrigan had also grown weary of the gypsy-like existence he had been leading from the start of spring training in February to the conclusion of postseason play in October. "Jumping all over the country seven months a year to keep up with baseball duties was all right when I was young and unattached," he said. "But now I was in my thirties, was married, and had an infant daughter. I wanted to spend more time with my family than baseball would permit," he explained. "So I retired."

Carrigan would not be the only big-name departure from the ball club that eventful off-season. Plagued by ill health and still smarting from the public criticism he had received for trading away Tris Speaker, Sox owner Joseph Lannin decided the time was right to call it quits and sell the team and ballpark. Regarding the latter, the Taylor family had earlier disposed of their Fenway holdings to Lannin after they had apparently grown tired of their landlord status. No matter. Lining up now to purchase both baseball properties for a

When the stylishly dressed thirty-six-year-old New York theatrical producer Harry Frazee purchased the team following the 1916 World Series, he promised to continue Boston's winning ways. "I have always enjoyed the game and now I think I shall have a chance to show what I know about handling a ball club," he said. (Courtesy of the Boston Red Sox.)

combined $675,000 was a stocky thirty-six-year-old New York theatrical producer named Harry H. Frazee.

"I think that by giving the public a first-class article I am bound to hold their support. And this goes double for Boston, which I consider, by all odds, the greatest ball town on earth," Frazee gleefully told a pack of reporters upon completion of the sale. There appeared no reason to doubt him, for "Frazz," as he was known to his closest associates, had always backed up such braggadocio with deeds. "He is a 'human dynamo' who will bring something in the way of activity and legitimate sensation [the sport] has never known before," the *Sporting News* reported. "He has ideas that in their working out will probably add an interesting chapter in the game's history."

Larry Gardner got a glimpse of just how "interesting" Frazee could be when he approached his new boss for a substantial pay raise prior to the start of spring training in 1917. "I felt I'd had a great year in 1916—batted over three hundred and hit two home runs in the Series," Gardner explained. But Frazee was not receptive, refusing to give an inch to his third baseman's salary request. "We argued for hours (I can still remember that little guy jumping up and down)," Gardner recounted, "and finally he said, 'I'll tell you what we'll do. We're training in Hot Springs [Arkansas] this year. You just got married. Bring your bride down there on the club.'"

Furious that he was unable to move Frazee one iota from his initial negotiating position, Gardner nevertheless found a way to get even. "I told my wife to take forty baths a day and ride horses the rest of the time. We really stuck Harry with that one!"

Frazee was usually not so easily bested. A tough and resourceful negotiator who quickly earned the reputation of being "the firebrand of the American League," he was not averse to taking big gambles. A case in point was his promotion of a series of vaudeville appearances for ex-heavyweight champion Jim Jeffries, who was preparing for his historic bout with the reigning African American boxing champ Jack Johnson in Reno, Nevada, in 1910. "Some of my friends told me this tour would be a failure, but I cleaned up $58,000 as my share of the profits," Frazee boasted afterward. But then, such financial risk-taking was in keeping with his overall philosophy of doing business. "No one ever made money in this world unless he took a chance," he said. "I was never afraid to play my one best bet for all I had." Frazee had developed this mindset early on in his life. A high school dropout, this hard-drinking and hard-living Peoria, Illinois, product had entered show business at the age of seventeen as a $40-a-week advance man for a touring stage company. He did this despite the misgivings of his parents, who no doubt would have preferred that he finish his education and enter a more conventional line of work. But conventionality had never been Frazee's strong point. He yearned to be a high roller and a force to be reckoned with in the theater world.

After years of toiling as a small-time producer, he finally achieved this lofty status in 1910 with the musical *Madam Sherry*. The box-office smash reportedly earned him a cool $250,000. Now the toast of Broadway, a financially flush Frazee went on to produce such popular hits as *A Pair of Sixes*, *A Full House*, and *Adele*. "He made more sense drunk than most people do sober," praised one contemporary.

In once trying to explain his success, Frazee was uncharacteristically modest. "My batting average hasn't been high," he conceded. "But I am satisfied. Here and there a play seems to catch on. What the public wants, it will pay for." To this end, he made a special point of churning out a large number of light comedies and musicals. "I go on the theory that people attend the theatre to be amused," he said. "I know that many go for instruction and for them, tragedies and Shakespeare are all well enough. But the rank and file go to the theatre for diversion, and I try to give them what they want. There are enough undertakers' announcements in the papers. Gaiety and life are in popular demand."

Baseball had always exercised a special hold on him. It's "the greatest amusement in the world," he once mused. "You forget everything else in the world when you are watching a game. That's why it has such a hold on people." After growing up an avid fan of the sport, he served a brief stint as manager of a barnstorming pro outfit out of Peoria. That experience proved to be far from edifying, however. "I wasn't a ballplayer and profited but little as a result of being known as manager," he said. Still, he enjoyed his time in the dugout enough to entertain thoughts of some day owning a team, if the right circumstances arose.

Lannin's abrupt decision to sell the Red Sox after the 1916 World Series provided him with just such an opportunity. Of course, it didn't hurt that the ball club he was purchasing was coming off back-to-back championships and was universally regarded as "the best supported club in either circuit and one of the best investments." To Frazee, that was just the cherry on top of the sundae. "I'm in the game for sport's sake," said the man who was ultimately destined to break the hearts of generations of New Englanders.

But before he trod down that dark path, he was hailed in most Beantown quarters as a savvy business operator who would keep the Red Sox in perennial pennant contention. "Like Joe Lannin," the *Boston Globe* exulted, "he is a fan 'from way-back' and that is reassuring to the fans of Boston and New England." Only Arthur Duffey of the *Boston Post* offered a cautionary note, suggesting that Frazee would have a tough time matching the high standards of excellence established by the previous ownership regime. "Boston fans," he wrote, "have become so accustomed to seeing championship teams here, and especially world's championship Red Sox team combinations, that they will not stand for anything less."

For his part, Frazee did not introduce any major changes to Boston's proven roster of talent when he first took over. Rather, he focused on trying to bring Carrigan back into the team's fold, even going so far as making a personal sojourn up to Lewiston, Maine, to change Carrigan's mind about retirement.

"We consider Bill Carrigan a great baseball manager," Frazee said, "and nothing will be left unturned to return Bill to the managership. . . . From all I can gather managers who rank better than Carrigan are few and far between." But this highly publicized full court press failed to reap dividends. "He made me a flattering offer and seemed very disappointed when I thanked him but said I was determined to stay out of the game," Carrigan related.

Undaunted, Frazee offered the vacated post to club second baseman Jack Barry, who immediately accepted. It was a popular move. Barry had been a key contributor on two Boston pennant winners and was well regarded by his peers in the game. "He knows baseball and don't think he doesn't," said Connie Mack, Barry's former manager. "I hated to see him leave the Athletics, but when he went to Boston I knew he would make good. He seems to have that disposition and temperament all essential to making good as a manager."

Barry himself expressed no doubt that he was ready to assume an expanded leadership role. "I want to tell the Boston fans that I will give all that's in me to the Red Sox and am sure of earnest support from every man on the team," he said.

Like the ball club he was inheriting, Barry knew a few things about winning. Recognized as one of the slickest fielders of his era, Barry had arrived in the majors in 1908, an unheralded twenty-year-old shortstop fresh off the campus of Holy Cross College in Worcester, Massachusetts. "You'll sit on the bench all summer and just observe," Connie Mack had informed him. But the discerning Athletics skipper soon realized what a rare talent he had in his possession and inserted the Meriden, Connecticut, native as a regular in the Philadelphia lineup. Mack was never given reason to regret his decision, later naming Barry to his all-time "Dream Team" in the late 1940s. "The Athletics have never had a shortstop to fill his shoes," he said.

Together with John "Stuffy" McInnis at first, Eddie Collins at second, and Frank "Home Run" Baker at third, Barry became the fulcrum of Mack's famed "$100,000 Infield," so named for the collectively high salaries they commanded. The unit proved to be worth every dime, however, as they led the Athletics to five AL pennants and three World Series championships during Barry's seven-and-a-half-year tenure with the club from 1908 to 1915.

Despite his knowledgeable hand at the team helm, Jack Barry could not duplicate Bill Carrigan's considerable success and deliver a third consecutive championship for Boston in 1917. (Courtesy of the Boston Red Sox.)

While the quiet and unassuming Barry refused to take any personal credit for Philly's success, his teammates and opponents were not as shy. "Play alongside Barry and you'll find that he is the best man playing the game," lauded Collins. "A lot of people are pulling for plays that I am supposed to make, handing out the salve to me when in reality it's Barry doing the work." Rival manager Hughie

Jennings of the Detroit Tigers preferred to focus on Barry's skill with the bat. While only a lifetime .243 hitter, "the Honus Wagner of the American League" had an uncanny ability to drive in runs in pressure situations. "In a pinch, Barry hits better than anybody in our league outside of Cobb," Jennings said.

Even Ty Cobb, never one to dispense compliments to opponents easily, had a grudging admiration for Barry. After spending years trying to cut down Barry in double-play situations, the fiery Detroit Hall of Famer once conceded that "this is one man I was sorry I spiked."

In spite of Barry's abilities, Boston was unable to win a third championship in a row in 1917. The Chicago White Sox, proving that their strong second-place finish of the previous year was no fluke, waltzed to the AL pennant with a franchise-best one hundred victories, nine games in front of the second-place Red Sox.

While both teams possessed strong pitching, Boston could not match the White Sox in terms of offense. Bolstered by the .300 hitting of "Shoeless" Joe Jackson and Hap Felsch, the Chicagoans led the junior circuit with 656 runs scored while batting a respectable .253. By way of comparison, Boston could only manage a somewhat lower .246 team average with 555 runs. Still, Red Sox fans were not without things to cheer about.

First and foremost, there was the continued pitching excellence of Babe Ruth. Cementing his reputation as the best left-hander in baseball, Ruth won a career-high twenty-four games as against thirteen losses for a robust .649 winning percentage. He also hurled six shutouts while completing an astonishing thirty-five games.

One of the few contests he was unable to finish that season, and one which earned him everlasting notoriety, occurred on June 23 against Washington. After walking lead-off man Eddie Foster, Ruth took umbrage at home plate umpire Brick Owens for his "ball and strike decisions." "Get back to your position, you big ape," Owens responded. When Ruth failed to take heed of this advice, Owens tossed him from the game, whereupon an enraged Ruth charged home and punched Owens in the face. "It wasn't a love tap, I really socked him—right on the jaw," Ruth said.

With his ace starter gone after pitching to only one batter, Barry elected to rush available right-hander Ernie Shore into the breach. "You see," Shore later told Donald Honig, "he never intended to have me go in there and finish the game. What he wanted me to do was go out on the mound and try to kill as much time as I could while he got somebody else ready in the bull pen."

As it turned out, Barry wouldn't need to dip into his relief corps. Shore, who would compile a respectable 13–10 record as a starter that year, did not allow any of the subsequent Washington batters he faced to reach base in what became the most unorthodox "perfect game" in major league history. "I don't believe I threw 75 pitches that whole game, if I threw that many," Shore said afterward. "They just kept hitting it right at somebody."

Given all the accolades Ruth and Shore received for their demonstrated heroics in 1917, it was easy to overlook the impressive pitching contribution of teammate Carl Mays. Having struggled to a decent but underwhelming 24–18 record in his first two seasons with Boston, Mays broke out with a superb 22–9 mark in 1917. In 289 innings pitched, he allowed just 230 hits while fanning ninety-one. None of this mattered much to the cantankerous Mays, however.

The son of an itinerant Methodist minister from the Midwest, Mays approached life with a sizable chip on his shoulder. "He was a real loner," said Larry Gardner. "I don't think he had a friend on the team." Always seeing enemies real or imagined around the corner, Mays had developed this paranoid mindset when he first entered the game.

"It was long ago made very apparent to me that I was not one of those individuals who were fated to be popular," he said. "It used to bother me some, for I suppose there are none of us who wouldn't prefer to be well thought of. But I was naturally independent and if I found that a fellow held aloof from me, I was not likely to run after him."

Indeed, Mays seemed to go out of his way in alienating team-mates, pointing out their individual flaws and telling them to their faces how they weren't putting out enough behind him on the field. "He was not congenial," remembered a former club member. "You would ask him a question and he would brush you off. I was never on a club that a fellow was disliked as much as Mays."

He "was simply an unlikable cuss, a pitcher opposing batsmen and teammates despised," maintains the author Donald Hubbard. Even the mild-mannered Miller Huggins, who would go on to manage Mays with some success with the Yankees in the 1920s, once confided to Frederick G. Lieb that of all his former charges, Mays was one of only two ballplayers he would ever turn down if they came to him for "a helping hand." "If they were in the gutter," Huggins said, "I'd kick them."

Pitcher Carl Mays: Perhaps one of the most hated figures in the game, the mercurial yet successful right hander had a penchant for alienating everybody, including his own teammates. He "wasn't very popular, but when nobody else could win Carl could," Duffy Lewis said. (Courtesy of the Library of Congress.)

One of Huggins's Yankees bosses, Tillinghast Huston, was not as virulent in his dislike of Mays, preferring to compare him to a man he once knew who had a special talent for pushing other people's buttons. "He hadn't a conspicuous fault that you could really put your finger on," Huston said. "But he antagonized everybody who came within the sound of his own voice. I knew him for what he was and yet in spite of it all he used to make me hot under the collar. One of the last times I was in his office, I felt so insulted that I got up and left. But when he later told me that I ought to know him better than to act that way, I knew he was right."

Ironically, Ty Cobb, who possessed an equal facility for estranging others, absolutely loathed Mays, perhaps demonstrating again the old maxim that alike people do indeed repel each other. But Cobb, being Cobb, took things a step further. When Mays once went to cover first base in a ballgame against the Tigers, the hard-charging Cobb viciously spiked him. "The next time you cover the bag," Cobb informed him, "I'll take the skin off your other leg."

Eventually things got so discouraging for Mays that he seriously contemplated leaving the game. Fortunately for him, he was talked out of it by his uncle. "In brief," Mays recalled, "he told me if I failed to make good, he would consider me a quitter and that is a word I never liked to take from any man."

The gloomy yet talented right-hander displayed a similar show of grit on the mound. He gave no quarter to the batters he faced with a deceptive, sweeping pitching motion that one scribe likened to "a cross between an octopus and a bowler." That same writer added that Mays "shoots the ball in at the batter at such unexpected angles that his delivery is hard to find, generally, until about 5 o'clock, when the hitters get accustomed to it—and when the game is about over."

Though he preferred to pitch tight inside and acquired a well-deserved reputation as a head hunter, Mays claimed that he never tried to hit anyone. "I throw close to keep the hitters close up there," he said. This approach proved successful. During his five years in a Boston uniform, he would average fourteen wins a season with an

ERA of slightly over two runs per contest. "He was a great stopper," Duffy Lewis said.

With the disappointing 1917 season behind them, the Red Sox eagerly looked forward to reclaiming top league honors in 1918. However, circumstances beyond their control appeared poised to thwart their chances. Due to the war raging in Europe, no less than eleven Sox players were called up for active military duty, including Duffy Lewis, Herb Pennock, Ernie Shore, and Jack Barry. "No club in either league has been so depleted by the war as have the Red Sox," the *Boston Globe* reported.

To make up for the talent shortfall, Harry Frazee embarked on an aggressive program of player acquisition. In short order, the Boston owner swung a pair of deals with Connie Mack's Philadelphia Athletics to acquire first baseman John "Stuffy" McInnis, outfielder Amos Strunk, pitcher "Bullet" Joe Bush, and catcher Wally Schang. In return, Frazee gave up very little, apart from a declining Larry Gardner, several reserve players, and $60,000 in cash.

"It makes the Hub Hose appear the strongest club 'on paper' in either league," opined Burt Whitman of the *Boston Herald*. Indeed, McInnis, Strunk, and Schang had all batted .280 or better the previous season, while Bush was a former sixteen-game winner who had memorably shut out the New York Giants 3–0 in game 3 of the 1913 World Series.

Still, Frazee was not satisfied. Seeing major holes to be filled at second base and left field, he traded for Cincinnati Reds veteran Dave Shean, a good no-hit infielder, and purchased George Whiteman, a career minor leaguer who had helped the Toronto Maple Leafs win the International League title in 1917. A decade earlier, Whiteman had been a promising outfield prospect with the Red Sox. "But I never got a show," the Peoria, Illinois, native later explained. "[Tris] Speaker didn't connect at first either, you may remember. But he got his chance and he sure made good. But I never seemed to get a chance, I was allowed to drift back to the minors and though I was signed several seasons later on, and played some

The acquisition of star pitcher "Bullet" Joe Bush from the Philadelphia Athletics helped secure the 1918 pennant for the Red Sox. (Courtesy of the Library of Congress.)

fourteen games with a fine batting average, I drifted back just the same. It seemed to be my luck."

One potentially rewarding and lucrative talent pool Frazee did not draw from was African American ballplayers. Owing to a so-called gentlemen's agreement that had been put in place among owners in professional baseball at the end of the nineteenth century, blacks were deliberately excluded from playing with whites in the majors. "My skin is against me," noted one frustrated black performer at the time.

This unofficial policy came into being largely due not only to the racist cultural attitudes that predominated in post-Reconstruction America but also to the efforts of Adrian "Cap" Anson, one of baseball's first superstars and the lead drawing card of the old Chicago White Stockings. An unabashed white supremacist who was not the least bit hesitant in expressing his hate-mongering views, Anson traded on his considerable standing in the game as a player and manager to block efforts at integration.

In 1887, for example, Anson flatly declined to allow his team to play a Toledo American Association club in an exhibition game solely because the players included a talented African American pitcher named George Washington Stovey. "Take him out or I get off," Anson said. "Anson's stand emboldened others in organized baseball to take a similar position," maintains historian Glenn Stout. Indeed, it now became the norm to shut out blacks from all big-league competition.

As one manifesto purportedly said to represent the majority view of the all-white St. Louis Browns put it, "We the undersigned members of the St. Louis Baseball Club do not agree to play against negroes. . . . We will cheerfully play against white people at any time, and think by refusing to play we are only doing what is right."

While Frazee liked to think of himself as a maverick operator, he did not possess the kind of personal courage or moral vision that pioneering executive Branch Rickey would later exhibit in forcing the integration of the game when he signed up Jackie Robinson for the

Brooklyn Dodgers in the 1940s. As a result, Frazee, even if he had seriously contemplated it, was of no mind to challenge the reigning status quo when it came to race. It would not be until 1959 that the Red Sox would actually have an African American on their major league roster, sadly the last team in professional baseball to do so.

As for the managerial vacancy created by Barry's departure, Frazee turned to Edward G. Barrow, a personal friend and baseball lifer who had served as president of the International League from 1911 to 1917. According to Barrow, he had been offered the job on the spot after paying a perfunctory social call on Frazee one afternoon.

"Did I want the job? I was so happy I couldn't answer," the surprised new Boston manager said. If true, this was probably one of the few instances where this pugnacious Wisconsin farmer's son was ever at a loss for words. "He was a big, broad-shouldered man who feared no one and could argue as forcefully with his fists as his tongue," *New York Times* sports columnist Arthur Daley once observed. "He was such a complete dictator that he merely had to utter, 'Close the window,' and subordinates fell over themselves to close the window."

Nor was he a very compassionate man. A worried ballplayer under his charge once asked him what he should do in the event Barrow cut him from the team roster. An unconcerned Barrow was blunt to the point of cruelty. "Well, I guess you're a dead one," he told the player. "And you know your life's history better than I do."

Accounting for this mean streak was an unhappy personal life. The product of a poor Nebraska farming family, Barrow had grown up used to poverty and bitter disappointment. When his father took ill, he had to drop out of school and take a job at a local roller-skating rink to support his family. He was also unlucky in love. An early marriage to a New York City stage performer by the name of Alice Calhoun proved ill advised and deeply painful. The union "was not a particularly blessed or lengthy one, and Barrow had little interest in reliving it later," biographer Daniel Levitt has written.

To cope with all these personal setbacks and failures, Barrow fortunately had the game of baseball to fall back on. The sport entered his life at a very young age. "I developed on the sand-lots, then pitched for my high school nine and for a Y.M.C.A team," Barrow later reminisced. "Soon I discovered my services were in local demand. But I got a bad break—or maybe it was a good one, as it ended my playing career. I pitched in a cold rain and developed neuritis in the arm. After that I pitched no more."

With his boyhood dream of becoming a major leaguer now shattered, he turned to the administrative side of the game for solace. At the age of twenty-six, he paired up with an up and coming sports concessionaire named Harry M. Stevens to purchase the Wheeling, West Virginia, club of the Inter-State League, a new minor league operation that had been conceived and organized by an Ohio sportswriter. Things went reasonably well until the middle of the 1895 season, when the league suddenly ran out of money and folded.

Unfazed, Barrow moved his club into the rival Iron and Oil League, where it promptly won the pennant. "One of my outfielders was Zane Grey," Barrow said. "He continued with baseball until he got to Washington, and then he had the sense to quit and go into writing those Western romances."

Barrow himself couldn't live without the game. In the decade and a half ahead, he continued to serve in a number of high-profile, baseball-related capacities, including field manager of the Detroit Tigers from 1903 to 1904. Although he improved the second division Tigers' overall win-loss record by an impressive thirteen games in his first season with the club, his imperious managerial style alienated his players and incoming Detroit owner Frank Navin. As a result, he was unceremoniously forced to step down from his post the following year.

Bitterly disappointed, Barrow later claimed that he had been the victim of an obdurate front office that had failed to provide him with the kind of players he needed to win ball games. This is why he fairly jumped at the chance to go to Boston, for Barrow believed that Frazee was providing him with a roster full of the kind of players he wanted, hard-nosed, established stars like McInnis, Strunk, Hooper, and Schang.

"There is every reason to believe the Red Sox will be in the hunt for the American League honors," the new Boston manager predicted. "We have a good ball club that has the ability to sail along once it strikes its stride. They are seasoned and many have been on championship clubs."

As if to prove the efficacy of Barrow's words, the Red Sox bolted out of the blocks once the regular season began, going a franchise-best 11–2 in April and easily securing first place. But the really big news coming out of Boston wasn't the winning streak but a $100,000 offer Frazee had reportedly turned down from an unnamed club for the pitching services of Babe Ruth. "The sum named was three times as much as was paid for Tris Speaker, and is far and away bigger than any figure that has been used in baseball. But it is ridiculous to talk about it. Ruth is our Big Ace. He's the most talked of, most sought for, most colorful player in the game," Frazee told the *Boston Herald*.

Whether this offer was genuine is unclear from existing sources. It wouldn't have been unlike Frazee, a showman at heart, to fabricate such a tale to extract some cheap publicity for his ball club. "You can't fill a theater with a poor attraction," Frazee once said. And no ballplayer had become a bigger attraction in the game than Ruth.

Coming off back-to-back twenty-win seasons, the "colossus," as the Boston press had begun to call Ruth, appeared primed for another standout year. Earning his third consecutive opening day start with the Sox on April 15, Ruth hurled a work of art. He mesmerized the visiting Philadelphians to the tune of four hits in a complete game, 7–1 victory at Fenway Park.

"It is the Babe's delight to take the joy out of things for ambitious ball clubs in the first game of the season," the *Boston Herald* said, as this was yet another example of how "the giant southpaw has whistled his way through to a win in the 'They're off' game." Ruth would record two more victories for the month, but his attention had already begun to drift away from the mound.

Feeling that he had the necessary skills to take the field as an outfielder when he wasn't pitching, Ruth badgered an initially resistant

Barrow to put him into games. "Barrow probably would have been committed someplace if he had worked a 23-game winner in the outfield when he still had such players as Duffy Lewis . . . on his team," Ruth later explained. "But 1918 was one of those makeshift seasons. It was like 1944 and 1945 during [World War II], when a manager had to make the best of the material he had left on his hands."

Indeed, with starting left fielder and right-handed hitter George Whiteman off to a mediocre start at the plate, Barrow took the attitude he had nothing to lose. He inserted the left-hand-hitting Ruth in Whiteman's place in the lineup against right-handers. The gamble paid off. Ruth would go on to hit an even .300 with 66 RBIs in 317 at-bats for Boston that year, while tying for the league lead in homers with eleven.

During the tumultuous 1918 season, Red Sox owner Harry Frazee told a Boston newspaper that he "might as well sell the franchise and the whole club as sell Ruth." That position would soon change. (Courtesy of the Library of Congress.)

"I was winning a lot of respect up there at the plate and getting the first of what turned out to be a record 2,056 bases on balls, most of them intentional," Ruth said. "And occasionally I was teeing off on that squash and getting distance which some of the sports writers of that era apparently found hard to believe."

Sports editor Burt Whitman of the *Boston Herald* believed that Ruth's performance in 1918 was nothing short of amazing. "Ruth is the large rumble in the Red Sox family," he wrote. "That [$100,000] valuation placed on the Big Fellow which owner Harry Frazee passed up without batting an eye does not seem far-fetched. Ruth's proving to be worth his weight in gold."

But with this success came problems. With every circuit clout Ruth made, his ego swelled accordingly. Never a big observer of club rules to begin with, the thrill-seeking slugger now seemed even worse, gambling, whoring, and drinking most of his nights away. "Babe was an irresponsible guy," remembered teammate Fred Thomas. "I'd never go out with him. He'd spend money all right, but he'd spend your money. He made more money than anybody but he never had any." It was perhaps then inevitable that he would clash with his straitlaced manager.

"Barrow was a strict disciplinarian," Ruth recalled. "I was still at the age when I resented anyone pulling too tight on me." Things came to a head on July 2 when Ruth took his time reporting to the clubhouse before a road game against the Senators. Barrow, whom Ruth dismissively referred to as "the old goddamn shitpot," read him the riot act, humiliating his star player before the entire assembled squad.

Barrow "gave me the worst bawling out of my entire career," Ruth confirmed. "It was a double-barreled beaut. He threatened to knock my block off." Infuriated by the verbal dress-down, Ruth stormed out of the clubhouse and informed the Boston media he was quitting the Red Sox to play for a semi-pro team owned by a shipbuilding company in Chester, Pennsylvania.

Frazee was not amused. "Ruth has signed a contract with the Boston club and must play baseball with us until that contract expires," the Sox chieftain thundered. "I shall notify both Ruth and [the Chester team] of this, and if they try to use him I shall get an injunction. . . . Ruth can't get away with it. The courts will not stand for a deal like that."

Ruth reached the same conclusion. He sheepishly rejoined the Sox on July 4 after missing only one game. "I'm sorry Eddie," he contritely told Barrow. "It won't happen again." To demonstrate that he meant it, he went out the next day and pitched the Sox to a 4–3 victory in extra innings over the cellar-dwelling Athletics on the road. The win couldn't have come at a better time.

After having led the AL for most of the season, Boston had lost six of their last ten games, falling a half-game behind Tris Speaker's Cleveland club in the standings. But with a chastened Ruth back in the fold, the team quickly regained its winning ways. Hosting the Indians at home, the Sox proceeded to take four out of the next five contests as "Big Babe" put on an offensive display. He "won three of the games single handedly," reported the *Herald*'s Eddie Hurley. "Twice he delivered triples in the pinch that robbed Cleveland of victory, and his wallop into the bleachers the other day [a 1–0 Boston victory in the second game of a July 9 doubleheader] tucked away another game. Today, Ruth is friendless in Cleveland."

Having regained first place from the Indians, the Sox held on the rest of the way to take the pennant by a comfortable margin over Cleveland. "Frazee was called the 'Red Sox wrecker' later on," Ruth later wrote of the man who traded him and several of his champion teammates to the Yankees, "but some of his war deals made our 1918 pennant possible." Specifically, the two earlier trades that had netted McInnis, Strunk, Schang, and Bush from the Athletics had made the most difference.

Bush won fifteen games and posted a club-leading 2.11 ERA with seven shutouts. Schang, a career .284 switch-hitter, proved a highly dependable backstop, compiling an outstanding .377 on-base percentage in eighty-eight games. McInnis, who hailed from nearby Gloucester on Boston's North Shore, finished second to Ruth in team

RBIs with fifty-six. Always fleet of foot, the former schoolboy stand-out, whose fierce competitive attitude once earned him the moniker of "wargod of the diamond," added to his fine showing at the plate by swiping ten bases. Strunk also relied on speed to lift his game. The Pennsylvania native, popularly known as "the Flying Foot," garnered twenty stolen bases to go with eighteen doubles and nine triples.

Nevertheless, these stellar performances might have all gone for naught if AL president Ban Johnson had gotten his way. In response to a July 19 directive from Secretary of War Newton Baker, which stated all ballplayers of eligible draft age had to "work or fight" in war-related enterprises, an overly reactive Johnson declared that the AL would be henceforward closed for business.

This announcement did not register well with either Ed Barrow or Harry Frazee. "The Boston American League club does not propose to abide by this arbitrary ruling," the former said. In point of fact, there wasn't much support among team owners or executives in either league for embarking on such an extreme course. Instead, a compromise deal spearheaded by Frazee was worked out with the War Department that permitted the regular season to continue until Labor Day and a World Series to be held shortly thereafter.

Although he greatly resented having his earlier decree rescinded, Johnson made a public show of supporting the new arrangement. He felt he had no other choice. "Johnson was angry," confirmed historian John P. Rossi, "but his protests were brushed aside by the owners seeking to salvage the rest of the season."

Never one to take a setback lightly, Johnson did manage to exact a small measure of revenge. Throwing established precedent to the wind, he scheduled the dates for the first three World Series contests outside "the home grounds of the American League pennant winners," with the remaining four, if necessary, to be played in Boston. Ostensibly this move was designed to cut down on wartime travel expenses, but in reality it was an unsubtle way of reminding Frazee who was still boss. His ball club would now be forced to play an additional road game out of the Series gate, a major competitive disadvantage. Unsurprisingly,

Frazee was irate, calling the move "unfair" and "an insult to Boston fans and to the best baseball town in the American League."

Insult or not, neither Frazee nor the Red Sox could afford to wallow in their misfortune, as they had a date with the formidable Chicago Cubs in the upcoming Fall Classic. A consensus pick to win it all, the Cubs had survived a late-season challenge by John McGraw's New York Giants to take the NL pennant by ten and one-half games. "My players are all set," manager Fred Mitchell confidently informed reporters on the eve of the Series.

To be sure, the club was solid from top to bottom and boasted a fine pitching staff led by southpaws Jim "Hippo" Vaughn (22–10) and George "Lefty" Tyler (19–9). At a commanding six feet, four inches, and 215 pounds, the side-winding Vaughn made for quite an intimidating presence on the mound. While he possessed a good fastball, he was not opposed to mixing things up to hitters with a stupefying

Chicago Cubs hurler Jim "Hippo" Vaughn: "Nothing pleased him better than to strike a man out pitching to his strength," said Grover Cleveland Alexander. (Courtesy of the Library of Congress.)

assortment of changeups. "Big Jim Vaughn used to pitch the particular kind of ball a batter liked best just to show that he couldn't hit it," remembered fellow pitcher Grover Cleveland Alexander.

Tyler, who had come up to the big leagues in 1910, was a native New Englander, having spent his youth learning the finer aspects of the game in Derry, New Hampshire. Widely regarded as "one of the most formidable left-handers in the National League," Tyler achieved pitching star status in 1914 when his sixteen victories helped propel an unheralded Boston Braves club to a surprise world championship. "Tyler hasn't the speed of Vaughn," noted one discerning writer. "He throws a sweeping outcurve ball, delivered with a cross-fire motion, a good slow ball and a better change of pace than Vaughn."

Offensively, the Cubs relied on the sturdy bats of rookie Charlie Hollocher and veteran outfielder Les Mann. Hollocher, who was praised as the greatest shortstop find "since Rabbit Maranville flashed over the baseball horizon," had a superlative year. He finished with a .316 batting average while topping the NL in hits (161), at-bats (509), and total bases (202).

"A yearling, but a wonder, this boy only three years ago was playing in the backlots of his native St. Louis," marveled the *Boston Globe*. "He has shown everything. He can hit, is a sensational fielder, fast base runner and smart as a steel trap." Hollocher would go on to hit .340 in 152 games in 1923 but then abruptly leave the sport a year later due to a bout with depression.

Though not as statistically impressive as his younger teammate, Mann nevertheless had his moments. The former Boston Brave and Federal League star batted .288 with fifty-five RBIs and a career-high twenty-one stolen bases. Yet it was his leadership ability in the clubhouse that drew the most raves. All season long, the *New York Times* reported, Mann "has displayed irrepressible enthusiasm and pep and has kept the players on the jump all the time. [His] personality has been a big help to the Cubs this year."

The earliest World Series on record kicked off on September 5 before an under-capacity crowd of nineteen thousand at Chicago's

Comiskey Park. Just a year earlier, the White Sox had attracted thirteen thousand more fans in the same ballpark for their Series opener against the Giants. Ironically, the Cub front office had rented out Comiskey in the mistaken belief that their smaller regular season home, Weeghmann Park (now Wrigley Field), would be more suitable to handle the expected crush of Series spectators. But times had changed. "War taxes, the high cost of living, the curtailed season and the shadow of the war accounts for the indifference of the public," reported the *Boston Globe.*

All the same, the Red Sox and Cubs staged an entertaining contest, one that saw the visitors secure a 1–0 victory behind the shutout pitching of starter Babe Ruth, a thirteen-game winner on the year. The big left-hander, who confided to a reporter beforehand that he'd "pitch the whole series, every game, if they'd let me," struck out four and allowed six hits in a complete game effort.

"Ruth had bewildering speed, a great curve and was as cool as a radiator in an apartment house," wrote Nick Flatley of the *Boston American.* "He worked the batters perfectly and . . . turned back the hostiles with consummate ease." His only real scare came in the bottom of the first when the Cubs loaded the bases with two outs. Facing batter Charlie Pick, a former Philadelphia Athletic who had hit .326 for Chicago in twenty-nine games, Ruth got him to fly out to left center to end the inning. "It was a corking drive but right straight into [Sox outfielder George] Whiteman's hands," lamented Chicago's Fred Mitchell afterward.

The Sox registered their lone run in the fourth when back-to-back singles by Whiteman and Stuffy McInnis scored Dave Shean, who had reached base on a walk issued by Cubs starter Hippo Vaughn (five hits and six strikeouts in nine innings). "We got the jump on them today," a relieved Sox skipper Ed Barrow said. "First blood counts for a lot in a short series. We knew Ruth was the man to beat the Cubs, and Babe came through as expected."

One area where the "Oriole boy" did come up short, however, was in the identity department. Prior to the game, Barrow had approached Ruth about watching his pitch selection to Chicago's Les Mann. "Now," Barrow warned, "this man is tough against left-handers, Babe, and any time he comes up in a pinch I want you to be careful. In fact, it won't do any harm to dust him off a bit, for he takes a heavy toe hold off the plate." Taking Barrow's words to heart, Ruth did exactly as instructed. When confronted with the batter he thought to be Mann at the plate in the first inning, Ruth proceeded to bean him in the forehead. Unfortunately, that person turned out to be Chicago right fielder Max Flack. "Babe, you wouldn't know General Grant if he walked up there with a bat," Barrow jokingly admonished his clueless star when he returned to the dugout.

An equally boisterous mood pervaded the ballpark during the seventh inning stretch. On an apparent whim, a brass band struck up "The Star Spangled Banner" to the express delight of the fans and players. Observed the *New York Times*, "First the song was taken up by a few, then others joined, and when the final notes came, a great volume of melody rolled across the field. It was at the very end that the onlookers exploded into thunderous applause and rent the air with a cheer." Boston third baseman Fred Thomas became so moved by the spontaneous show of patriotism that he "stood at attention in a military salute." Thus, a time-honored baseball tradition was born. Eventually, teams across the land would make the singing of the "National Anthem" an accepted staple at every ballgame.

Bullet Joe Bush drew the starting assignment against Chicago's Lefty Tyler for game 2 amid the soaring expectations of his team-mates that he would give the Sox a 2–0 lead in the Series. Barrow was chiefly to blame for creating this smug mindset. Just prior to the game, he informed his club that Tyler would be far easier to beat than Hippo Vaughn as the former lacked the same kind of explosive speed. "We're sure to get Tyler," he said.

This appraisal notwithstanding, Tyler came out on the winning end of a tightly contested 3–1 decision. Indeed, the Chicago curveballer was just shy of brilliant, outdueling Bush and limiting the Boston attack to six scattered hits over nine innings. "The task of the Cubs is now easier," Fred Mitchell said. "We are now on even terms with Boston."

All of the Cubs runs came in the bottom of the second inning. Bush issued a lead-off walk to Cubs first baseman Fred Merkle, who advanced to second when a Charlie Pick grounder got misplayed for a hit by the Boston infield. One out later, Merkle scored on a first pitch swinging double to right by Cubs catcher Bill Killefer. Pick went to third on the play, setting the stage for the weak-hitting Tyler, batting ninth, to become the game's unlikely offensive star. After taking a called strike, the Cubs hurler drew a bead on a "perfect" Bush fastball down the middle of the plate and crushed it. "The Red Sox infield was drawn in close [for a potential play at the plate] and the ball bounded by Bush into centre, Pick and Killefer scoring," the *Boston Herald*'s Burt Whitman wrote.

The Boston lineup meanwhile had no answer for Tyler's repertoire of off-speed pitches until the bottom of the ninth. Lead-off man Amos Strunk got on board with a standup triple into the right-field corner. George Whiteman then followed with a three-bagger of his own, an authoritative drive to center that drove in Strunk. But there the abortive Sox rally ended. Tyler regained enough of his pitching rhythm to record the final three outs, including a big strikeout of Sox pinch hitter Jean Dubuc, whose specialty was torching left-handed pitchers. "Today's game was a tough one, especially as we nearly broke it up in the ninth inning," Barrow conceded. "The Cubs had the better of the breaks, I think, and piled up a lead in the second inning too great for us to overcome."

Adding to the drama on the field was a fist-fight between Heinie Wagner and Chicago third base coach Otto Knabe, who was known in baseball circles as "the official barker of the Cubs." Following Chicago's offensive explosion in the second inning, Wagner and Knabe exchanged some heated words that led to the two of them squaring off under the stands.

"If you wanna fight, you dirty bastard, let's go right now," Wagner reportedly said. The fracas ended when players from the Cubs dugout arrived on the scene to break it up. However, there was no question as to who got the better of whom in this impromptu skirmish. "The chunky Knabe upset Wagner and mopped up considerable dirt with the broad back of the Boston coach," wrote Charley Dryden in the *Boston American*.

No further tussles broke out in game 3, though surprise Cubs starter Hippo Vaughn might have been tempted to take a swing or two at his teammates. Working on a single day's rest, Vaughn once again pitched well enough to win (seven strikeouts and seven hits allowed) but was let down by an anemic home offense in a 2–1 loss to Carl Mays. "I thought Vaughn would beat them sure," Fred Mitchell commented, "but it seems we can't get any runs for him."

Mays, who had recorded a 21–13 record during the regular season, may have had something to do with that. Though erratic at times, the scrappy Kentuckian was able to stay out of major trouble with a baffling array of sidearm offerings that kept Cub batters off balance all afternoon. At one point, he even retired ten in a row. He "always had the hostiles under control," wrote the *American*'s Nick Flatley. The Cubs did scratch out a run in the bottom of the fifth on a RBI single by Bill Killefer, but that was the extent of their scoring output. "We had no luck and no good breaks," Mitchell complained.

Instead, all the breaks seemed to go Boston's way, with the fourth inning being a prime example. With one out and a man on second, Cubs outfielder Dode Paskert tagged a Mays pitch to deep left center that had everyone in the ballpark thinking two-run homer. That is, until George Whiteman came streaking out of nowhere to make a spectacular, leaping grab. "It was a sweet catch," noted the *Boston Globe*'s Edwin Martin, "for the ball stood a fine chance of bounding into the bleachers for a circuit knock."

Good fortune was also on Boston's side in the ninth when a Mays pitch got away from catcher Wally Schang with two down and the Cubs' Charlie Pick on second. Pick immediately broke for third and was called safe by umpire George Hildebrand as Schang's accurate return throw was dropped by Sox third baseman Fred Thomas.

But instead of "getting the ball as quickly as possible," wrote Burt Whitman, "[Thomas] started to expostulate to Hildebrand, claiming that Pick had intentionally knocked the ball out of his hand." Sensing an opportunity, Pick raced for home, only to be cut down at the plate by "an unerring, rapid-fire peg" from Thomas, who had wisely elected to end his quarrel with Hildebrand. "We took a desperate chance and lost," Mitchell said.

As in game 2, the Sox scored all their runs in the fourth. The rally started when Whiteman got plunked in the ribs by a Vaughn curve and was awarded first base. McInnis moved him over to second on a two-strike hit that was as improbable as it was timely. "Well, that was supposed to be a beanball," Vaughn confessed to reporters afterward. "I got the first two pitches past McInnis for strikes. I wanted to drive him back from the plate, so I intended to shoot the next close to his bean. My control was bad, and I got it almost over the plate just where he likes 'em, and he hit it to left field."

Schang, the next Boston batter, made Vaughn pay for the mistake by singling to center, scoring Whiteman and advancing McInnis to third. From there, things went further awry for the Cubs left-hander, as he allowed Everett Scott to get off a successful squeeze bunt that drove in McInnis for Boston's second and final run. "It was my fault," Vaughn said. "[My teammates] gave me one run and that should have been enough for us to win."

Having taken two out of three games from the Cubs in their own backyard, the Red Sox were understandably in a jubilant mood as they entrained to Boston for the remaining Series contests. But this happiness soon turned to sullen resentment when the players learned that their postseason cash allotments would be far smaller than expected.

Earlier in the year, AL and NL owners had gotten together to decree that World Series participants would hereafter have to "divide [their share] of the prize money among the players on the teams which finished second, third, and fourth" in their respective leagues during the regular season. "We felt that was all right, but not under wartime conditions, when baseball salaries were off," Babe Ruth later wrote.

To address the situation, the team made common cause with the Cubs and sent a delegation of players headed by Harry Hooper and Les Mann to meet with the National Commission. Their goal was to convince the ruling baseball body that it should either "hold back the purses to first-division players in 1918, or give a flat sum of $1500 to the winning players in the World Series and $1000 to the losers." But the commission refused to meet with the delegation, thus making an already acrimonious situation even worse.

As if there wasn't already enough excitement, Ruth chose this precise moment to injure his throwing hand, thereby jeopardizing his status as the scheduled Boston starter for game 4. Ruth later claimed he and teammate Walt Kinney, a seldom used reserve pitcher, were engaged in a friendly bit of "roughhousing" aboard one of the Michigan Central train cars that had been specially commissioned to bring the Sox and Cubs back to Boston. "I took a swing at Kinney, but he ducked and I hit my knuckles of my left hand on the steel wall of the car," Ruth recalled. "The middle finger of my left hand became swollen to three times its normal size."

Another version of events had Ruth being the victim of a sudden lurching of the train, which sent him, according to one newspaper account, "aspinning and crashing against a window." Regardless of the cause, Ruth was hurt and this launched Barrow into a blistering rage. "You damn fool," the Boston manager told Ruth. "You know you're supposed to pitch . . . and you go fooling around like this."

In spite of the injury, Ruth gamely took the mound for game 4 the next afternoon at Fenway. But from the outset, he realized something was seriously wrong. "The swollen finger prevented me from getting my regular grip on the ball," he confessed. "I couldn't get the right twist when I threw my curve." The Cubs, however, failed to capitalize, as they wasted another fine pitching performance from Lefty Tyler (two earned runs on seven hits in seven innings) and lost 3–2. "To win [the Series] now," the *Boston Herald* reported,

"Chicago must take three straight from the Bostonians, and all the games must be played at Fenway Park. Truly an impossible task for the National League titlists."

And Ruth was mainly responsible for putting them in that situation. In making his second Series start after only three days of rest, he held the Cubs to a mere seven hits and hurled shutout ball through the first seven innings. In the process, he extended his postseason scoreless innings streak to twenty-nine and two-thirds, a pitching record that would stand until 1961 when Whitey Ford broke it, and one that the future home-run king labeled his "proudest achievement" in the game. "It beat that of the great [Christy] Mathewson, who pitched 28 consecutive World Series innings, 27 of them in his three shutouts against the Athletics in 1905 and one more inning against the A's in 1911," Ruth boasted.

Ruth also hit a bases-clearing triple in the home half of the fourth that gave the Sox an early 2–0 lead. "Tyler tried to slop a fast one past Ruth," the *Boston Post's* Paul Shannon wrote. "A report like a rifle shot rang through the park. Twenty-five thousand people arose as one man, and while the bleachers shrieked in ecstasy, the Cubs right fielder dashed madly for the centre field stands while two red-legged runners scampered about the bases. The sphere sailed over [Max] Flack's head on a line, dropped at the foot of the bleachers, and before the relayed throw was rescued near the Cub dugout two runs had come in for Boston, and the big pitcher was resting on third."

The Cubs came back to tie the game in the eighth after a tiring Ruth gave up two hits, a walk, and a wild pitch. But the Sox responded with a rally of their own in the bottom frame. Wally Schang led off with a base hit to center which he was subsequently able to score on when the Chicago reliever and celebrated spitball artist Phil Douglas botched a routine sacrifice bunt by Harry Hooper down the third base line. "It was a spitter, and when the big twirler hurled it to first base it sailed away over Fred Merkle's head," Shannon noted. "Schang ran home and the fate of the contest was decided."

Fate had nothing to do with the tumultuous events that preceded the start of game 5. Upset that their concerns about smaller World Series shares had been ignored by upper management, Red Sox and Cubs players collectively decided to stage a boycott of the contest just as the ballpark was filling up with eager fans. Needless to say, this provocative action irritated the ruling baseball powers-that-be, most notably Ban Johnson, who had arrived at the ballpark in a thoroughly intoxicated state.

"If [we] concede anything to those pups," he exclaimed, "I'm through with baseball. I'm through. I'm through. I'm through." This intractable attitude notwithstanding, Johnson and his fellow National Commission members Garry Herrmann and John Heydler did agree to meet with representatives of the striking players in a hastily arranged airing-out session in the Fenway umpires' room.

What followed did little to dispel the bad blood that already existed between the two camps. Begging player spokesman Harry Hooper to end the walkout, Johnson insisted that both ball clubs had a moral obligation to take the field, regardless of how poorly they felt they were being financially compensated. "There are going to be wounded soldiers and sailors at the game again today," he said. "With a war going on, and fellows fighting in France, what do you think the public will think of you ballplayers striking for more money?"

Frustrated that he was getting nowhere with the commissioners and fearful that the players themselves would be made to look like greedy ingrates, Hooper yielded to Johnson's dramatics, albeit with the tacit understanding that no reprisals would be taken against his teammates or any of the Cubs. "We will play," he announced, "not because we think we are getting a fair deal. Because we are not. But we'll play for the sake of the game, for the sake of the public, which has always given us its loyal support, and for the sake of the wounded soldiers and sailors who are in the grandstand waiting for us."

While most of the twenty-five thousand fans in attendance initially viewed the strike with bitter resentment, going so far as to call the players "Bolsheviki," their attitude assumed a far different aspect

A thoroughly intoxicated Ban Johnson tearfully pleaded with player spokesman Harry Hooper to end a joint Red Sox-Cubs labor walkout before the start of game 5. (Courtesy of the Boston Public Library, T. "Nuf Ced" McGreevey Collection.)

A personally disgusted Hooper caved in to Johnson's histrionics. "We will play . . . for the sake of the public, which has always given us its loyal support, and for the sake of the wounded soldiers and sailors who are in the grandstand waiting for us." (Courtesy of the Boston Red Sox.)

once it became clear that the game would be played. As the *Chicago Tribune* reported, "When the players came on the field an hour late some of the fans started 'booing' them, but the majority cheered the athletes and drowned out the boos." Former Boston mayor and Red Sox devotee John "Honey Fitz" Fitzgerald provided a big assist here. The popular pol had earlier marched to home plate with a megaphone in hand to announce that the Red Sox and Cubs had "agreed to compete only for the good of the game and the public." "There is no doubt," the *Boston Record* said, "the players would have been given all the worst of it [if Honey Fitz hadn't intervened]."

In contrast to all the pregame excitement, the contest itself proved to be relatively uneventful. Hippo Vaughn, Chicago's hard-luck loser from games 1 and 3, shut out the Red Sox 3–0 on five hits to notch his only complete game victory of the Series. "I didn't have so much stuff today as I had in my first appearance," Vaughn said. "And I didn't pitch so good a game. But I won. The games have been so close that a single badly pitched ball has decided every one of them."

The Cubs recorded their first run in the top of the fourth when Les Mann doubled home Charles Hollocher, who was a perfect three for three with a walk against losing Sox pitcher Sad Sam Jones (three earned runs on seven hits). Jones "failed to stop the rejuvenation of Chicago's batsmen," noted the *New York Times*, "and they merrily thumped their hits out in effective groups." In the seventh, Dode Paskert added to the Cubs lead with a two-run double off the left-field wall that essentially put the game out of reach for Boston.

Not that they were ever really in it. The listless Sox lineup, which ended up hitting an embarrassing .186 for the Series, produced no base runners who advanced beyond second the entire contest. A good showing it wasn't, but in defeat a disappointed Ed Barrow tried to keep things in proper perspective. "We expected to end it today," he said, "but things broke too well for Chicago. So we'll win tomorrow with Mays or Bush."

Yet who would emerge as the victor of the Series had now become immaterial in the eyes of many seasoned baseball observers. The short-lived players strike "under the sinister shadow of the dollar sign" had seen to that. "It's a mighty good thing that professional baseball is dead," the *Post*'s Arthur Duffey wrote. "The game has been dying for two years, killed by the greed of the players and owners."

While an exaggeration, such disillusionment did contribute to the low fan turnout of fifteen thousand for game 6 the following afternoon. As the *Globe* reported, "Cold weather influenced many people not to attend the final game, but what kept many fans away was the hour's delay before [yesterday's] game, while the players and the commission tossed out ultimatums at each other."

Despite the lack of hometown support, the Sox still possessed enough mettle to defeat the Cubs 2–1 while earning world championship honors for the fifth time in less than two decades. "They must be given credit," the *Boston American*'s Eddie Hurley wrote. "They went through the season intact in the face of more upsets and more unpleasantness than was ever the lot of a championship team before. They've got the stuff that makes heroes. Is it any wonder they won?"

George Whiteman got the Boston victory express rolling in the bottom of the third. Squaring off against Chicago's Lefty Tyler with two down and teammates Carl Mays and Dave Shean in scoring position, Whitey tagged a screaming liner toward Cubs outfielder Max Flack in right. "Flack," reported the *Post*'s Paul Shannon, "who was playing well out, tore in to catch the liner. He reached it by a desperate sprint, but the ball had been driven with such force that it tore his hands apart and dropped to the ground while Shean followed Mays across the plate."

The Cubs got a run back the following inning on a RBI single by Fred Merkle, but from there their offense sputtered to a halt as Boston starter Carl Mays exerted total mastery, giving up three hits in nine complete innings. "Carl Mays tickled their knees and shins with low sweeping curves which saved Umpire George Hildebrand from dusting off the plate all afternoon," the *New York Times* said. "[His] pitching was tricky and tantalizing and the Chicago stickers spent most of the time rolling the ball along the infield."

Unlike their previous World Series wins, however, there was very little celebrating done on the Red Sox side. The team's humiliation at the hands of Ban Johnson and the National Commission the day before had evidently dampened their enthusiasm for such a "wild demonstration of joy." But one Boston player could not help but revel in the team's victory.

After toiling so many years in the minors, George Whiteman had seen just about everything there was to see in the game. Except this. "It came late, but I got my chance at last," a beaming Whiteman said afterward. "I was sure I could [make] good and I guess I have." Indeed, the amiable Texan had become the "hero of the Series" by tying Stuffy McInnis for the team lead in hits with five and playing a standout left field. "Harry Hooper, himself, from whom great deeds in the field are taken as a matter of course, could not have improved upon Whiteman's work in the gardens," wrote F. C. Lane of *Baseball Magazine*.

Unfortunately for Whiteman, he would not have anything tangible to show for his club's triumph over the Cubs. That's because the National Commission had peremptorily decided to deny Boston the diamond-encrusted emblems that customarily went to World Series victors. "Owing to the disgraceful actions of the players in the strike during the Series," the commission said, "each member of the team is fined the Series emblems." In the decades to follow, many players, including Whiteman, initiated efforts to see this punitive and arbitrary action overturned, but to no effect.

Major league baseball held firm in supporting the commission's original ruling. That is, until 1993 when the Red Sox organization sought and received the official go-ahead to finally recognize the 1918 champs during a special awards ceremony at Fenway Park. While no member of the team was still alive, enough of their descendents were around to posthumously accept replica emblems on their behalf.

"I want to thank the Red Sox for taking this step," remarked an emotional John Hooper. "All through the years my Dad, Harry

Hooper, made requests to every baseball commissioner to get medals awarded to the players, realizing that many of them would have no further chance to get such an award. Now the Red Sox have shown the courage and consideration to see that the medals are awarded."

For George Whiteman and his 1918 teammates, it was an honor long overdue.

CHAPTER SIX
COLLAPSE, RENEWAL, AND LEGACY (1919–2004)

Exactly two months after the last out had been recorded in the 1918 World Series, the Great War ended. A bankrupt and militarily exhausted Germany was forced to sign an armistice with the victorious Allies on November 11. In America, a collective sigh of relief was released throughout the entire nation. More than one hundred thirty thousand American soldiers had been killed in the conflict and another two hundred thousand had been wounded.

"The Americans who went to Europe to die are a unique breed," President Woodrow Wilson said. "Never before have men crossed the seas to a foreign land to fight for a cause which they did not pretend was peculiarly their own, which they knew was the cause of humanity and mankind. These Americans gave the greatest of all gifts, the gift of life and the gift of spirit."

Now it was all over and the business of building a durable peace was at hand. But revolutionary violence abroad in tandem with massive labor and racial strife at home, a sharp economic downturn, and a deadly outbreak of Spanish influenza soon conspired to blast such hopes. Nor was Wilson himself spared. Shortly before being incapacitated by a paralyzing stroke, he unsuccessfully labored to have his dream of a "peace without victory" realized. This meant no Carthaginian terms imposed on a vanquished Germany. But fellow

175

Allied partners David Lloyd George of Great Britain and Georges Clemenceau of France saw things differently.

Their respective countries had expended even greater blood and treasure than the United States during the war, and they were not of the mind to let Germany off the hook. Put another way, they wanted to squeeze their old enemy "until the pips squeak." As a result, Germany was forced to humiliatingly give up huge chunks of its own territory, cough up billions of dollars in war reparations, and accept a specially drawn up statement of "war guilt" for having supposedly caused the conflict in the first place. Thus the seeds for a far greater and more terrible war down the road were planted. Instead of the "normalcy" everyone craved, Americans found only disillusionment, upheaval, and the election of Warren G. Harding as president.

An underlying sense of unease also extended to the 1919 baseball season. While the Red Sox had the bulk of their championship roster returning, they were minus a pair of key performers. Bullet Joe Bush, who had pitched a workhorse total of 273 innings in 1918 to go along with a team-leading 2.11 ERA, came down with an arm injury that kept him out for most of the year.

World Series hero George Whiteman also went MIA, but his status had nothing to do with a physical malady. Sox management branded the outfielder redundant once it had again signed up Harry Hooper that spring. Although Whiteman would kick around organized ball for another eleven years, he would never again play in the majors.

Despite these personnel losses, the Sox were picked by most prognosticators to repeat as AL champs. "Under no conditions in a league stronger than ever, can the Sox make a runaway race of it," wrote Burt Whitman of the *Boston Herald*. "But they have the elements of victory and will win under [manager Ed] Barrow's leadership, if the pitching staff comes through."

To be sure, with Carl Mays and Babe Ruth at the top of the rotation, the team appeared to have the strongest pitching staff in baseball. But it lacked offensive punch and, most important of all, depth. Harry

Frazee hadn't helped matters in the off-season when he traded away returning service vets Ernie Shore and Duffy Lewis along with Dutch Leonard to the Yankees for four lesser players and $25,000 in cash.

All three had been major contributors on past Boston championship squads, but only Leonard had seen any appreciable playing time since 1917. Frazee deemed them "expendable" and few in Boston took serious issue. Still, their savvy veteran leadership and proven skills on the field might have come in handy once the Sox stumbled out of the gate in 1919. For the club was a major disappointment. Saddled with a subpar pitching performance from Mays and unable to score runs consistently as a team, the defending champs collapsed into sixth place by the close of May.

With the club sputtering to an early exit from the pennant race, most fans focused their attention on Ruth, who began hitting home runs at an unprecedented rate. By July, he had already matched his entire 1918 output with eleven, despite continuing to divide his playing time between the pitcher's mound and the outfield. "It was rough," Ruth later admitted.

Fortunately, he had teammate Harry Hooper watching his back. The highly respected veteran approached Barrow and told him in plain terms that the team was better off with Ruth getting his at-bats on an everyday basis. "All right," a skeptical Barrow reportedly responded, "I'll put Ruth out there, but mark my words, after the first slump he gets into, he'll come back on his knees begging to pitch again."

The latter scenario never developed, but Ruth's fielding skills were another matter altogether. He "sure wasn't a born outfielder," Hooper confessed. "I was playing center field myself, so I put the Babe in right field. On the other side of me was a fellow named Braggo Roth, another wild man. I'd be playing out there in the middle between these two fellows and I began to fear for my life. Both of them were galloping around that outfield without regard for life or limb, hollering all the time, running like maniacs after every ball. A week of that was enough for me. I shifted the Babe to center and I moved to right, so I could keep clear of those two."

Although the Red Sox faltered in the standings, Babe Ruth broke the individual home run record with twenty-nine blasts in 1919. Nevertheless, this singular accomplishment did not prevent owner Harry Frazee from shipping him off to the Yankees in the off-season. (Courtesy of the Library of Congress.)

At last freed from the physical and mental demands of having to pitch every fourth day, Ruth soared to even greater heights as a hitter. He batted well above .300 and continued to launch balls into the stratosphere. "Ruth is far and away the hardest hitter of all time, in my opinion," gushed former NL pitching star Clark Griffith. "He is not so consistent a batter as many I have faced. But when he connects, the ball goes farther. I am going to be pulling for him to beat Buck Freeman's old home-run record."

Freeman had hit twenty-five round-trippers for the Washington Senators back in 1889, establishing what was believed to be the all-time mark for homers in a single season. Ruth exceeded this total on September 8, when he deposited a curve delivered by Yankee left-hander Herb Thormahlen into the right-field grandstand of the Polo Grounds during the eighth inning of a 3–1 Boston victory. "It was not one of those fluke affairs which just managed to tumble into the stands," noted one newspaper account. "The ball kept rising as it traveled and when it banged into the seats in the farthest corner it was still going upward. It crashed among the excited fans."

When it was revealed shortly thereafter by an intrepid statistician that the real record was twenty-seven homers set by infielder Ed Williamson of the Chicago NL Club in 1884, Ruth barely missed a beat. "I was getting hotter and hotter," he explained later, "and on September 20th I tied Williamson's mark [at home] when I drove a long homer off Lefty Williams, the little White Sox southpaw, who was later tossed out of the game in the Black Sox scandal."

Ironically, the Black Sox scandal Ruth referred to got its ignominious start later that same day when Chicago first baseman Chick Gandil huddled with known gambler and lowlife Joseph "Sport" Sullivan at the Buckminster Hotel down the street from Fenway Park. There they hatched a scheme that would eventually implicate seven other White Sox players, including hitting great "Shoeless" Joe Jackson. Their plot called for the dumping of World Series games in that year's Fall Classic against the Cincinnati Reds. "Yeah—we were crooked," fellow conspirator Ed Cicotte admitted.

Fixing games, of course, was nothing new in professional baseball. Over the years, players had frequently tanked contests to win lucrative wagers or to supplement the relatively meager salaries they received from parsimonious management, which often seemed to take perverse delight in low-balling their undervalued employees.

Star infielder Hal Chase of the New York Yankees was among the most notorious of these cheats. Possessing what one sports editor called "a corkscrew brain," Chase was believed to have thrown many a ballgame through a steady procession of timely defensive lapses, despite sporting the reputation of being the finest fielding first baseman of his era. It "would take a suspicious-minded person," wrote Frederick G. Lieb, "to charge him with anything but an error if a well-thrown peg slipped off the end of his glove." But slip away they invariably did.

Significantly, these kinds of planned fielding miscues had occurred mostly in meaningless regular season games, not on the sport's greatest competitive stage and showcase. That's why when the Black Sox scandal first went public in the fall of 1920 following an official grand jury inquiry, most of the nation was placed in a state of shock and mortification. And no one was more flabbergasted by the news than Babe Ruth. "It was like hearing that my church had sold out," he said.

But that was all in the future. By the end of the 1919 season, Ruth had managed to hit two more homers, giving him twenty-nine on the year along with the distinction of having eclipsed Williamson's thirty-five-year-old record. For this feat, he became not only the game's most prolific slugger but also a certifiable "superstar."

As Melville E. Webb Jr. of the *Boston Globe* had observed early on in the home-run chase, Ruth "is the greatest drawing card in either league. He has outshone even 'Ty' Cobb in this respect. The fans love a great hitter, but they pretty much adore this fellow, who, when he comes to bat, causes the fielders to back away toward the boundaries and then proceeds to aim his blows at districts well beyond the limits of the playing field."

Despite Ruth's batting heroics, the Sox could not reverse their long, inexorable slide in the standings, finishing in sixth place, twenty and a half games out. The climax to this "lost season" occurred during a July 13 game in Chicago. Having been roughed up for four runs by the White Sox in the first two innings, temperamental pitching ace Carl Mays decided he had had enough and refused to return to the mound in the third. "Tell Barrow I've gone fishing," he angrily instructed a teammate in the clubhouse.

What apparently had set Mays off was a series of fielding miscues that his defense had made behind him, including a botched double-play ball. While Chicago went on to win the contest 14–9, the final outcome was of little concern to Mays. "I'll never pitch another ball for the Red Sox," he told the *Boston Herald* the next day. "I intend to fix up my affairs here and then go fishing in Pennsylvania."

When pressed to explain his extreme behavior, Mays, who was sporting an uncharacteristically poor 5–11 record, pointed to the standings. "The entire team is up in the air, and things have gone from bad to worse," he said. "The team cannot win with me pitching so I am getting out. And that's all there is to it."

Sox management was more than happy to oblige Mays's trade demand, as it had come to view the talented yet headstrong right-hander as "a chronic malcontent." A league-wide bidding war for Mays's services thus began. The pennant-bound White Sox reportedly offered Frazee some $30,000 in cash. But the Yankees, who were then battling with Chicago and Cleveland for the league lead, were not to be denied. Under the dynamic ownership team of Jacob Ruppert and Tillinghast Huston, they put in a winning bid of $40,000 along with two mid-level pitching prospects.

Getting what they wanted was nothing new to Ruppert and Huston. Since taking over the Yankees in 1914, they had transformed the ball club from a perennial second division finisher into a serious pennant threat. A born aristocrat, Ruppert spent most of his time tending to the family business, which was a highly profitable brewery in New York City that produced "Knickerbocker" beer. Imperious in manner and appearance, this "Prince of Beer" seemed to take great pleasure in intimidating his employees and other perceived inferiors. He "rode in a Pierce-Arrow the size of a Pullman car, all gleaming bright as if it had been bought new that morning,"

The 1919 season would be Carl Mays's last in a Red Sox uniform. He would end up with the Yankees and pitch several more productive years. He would also gain everlasting infamy for killing Cleveland's Ray Chapman with a pitch in 1920. (Courtesy of the Library of Congress.)

remembered Waite Hoyt, who would join the Yankees in 1921. "Once in a while he would take a few of us to the ballpark in it and would try to discuss with us the team's prospects and even make mild jokes at our expense."

Unlike his business partner, Huston had not inherited his fortune. A veteran of the Spanish-American War, he had struck it rich as a civil engineer in Cuba. "He was a big heavy man, a careless dresser, open and friendly, who considered the ballplayers and sportswriters his friends," noted the historian Robert W. Creamer.

Of the two, Ruppert was clearly the dominant partner, owing to his superior wealth and connections. But neither his wealth nor his connections could have prepared him for the public firestorm that was about to erupt over the Mays trade.

Determining that Frazee's failure to punish Mays for his controversial walkout would set "a bad precedent" in all future player-management relations, iron-fisted AL boss Ban Johnson decided to scuttle the trade. "Baseball cannot tolerate such a breach of discipline," he declared. "It was up to the owners of the Boston club to suspend Carl Mays for breaking his contract, and when they failed to do so, it is my duty as head of the American League to act. Mays will not play with any club until the suspension is raised. He should have reported to the Boston club before they made any trade or sale."

Chafing under this imposed restriction, Ruppert sought and received an injunction from Justice Robert L. Bruce of the Supreme Court of the State of New York "restraining President Ban Johnson of the American League from interfering with the performance of the contract between the Yankees and Carl W. Mays." A flurry of lawsuits between Johnson and Ruppert ensued. But in the end, Ruppert prevailed in the courts and Mays was allowed to pitch for the Yankees.

As for Johnson, he suffered a major blow to his authority as baseball's reigning "czar." Long simmering resentment against his autocratic ways now broke out into the open. Indeed, the league splintered into two opposing factions: the "Loyal Five" (Cleveland, Detroit, St. Louis, Philadelphia, and Washington) who supported

Johnson and the "Insurrectos" (Boston, Chicago, and New York) who did not.

Frazee, in particular, harbored strong feelings against Johnson, as he had been deeply chagrined by the latter's willingness to shut down the 1918 season during the wartime emergency. "I rather like to manage my own business, but if I can't, I at least want to be consulted," Frazee fumed. "If someone puts a sign on my park, closed for the season, I insist on being one of the innocent bystanders to watch the proceedings."

Frazee and the Insurrectos eventually carried the day when the Loyal Five forsook Johnson in the wake of the Black Sox scandal. They believed the longtime power broker had lost his effectiveness, as evidenced by his inability to forestall such an embarrassing event. They desired change, and that meant, according to historian Geoffrey C. Ward, dissolving "the old three-man National Commission run by Ban Johnson that had overseen the game in favor of a single, independent commissioner, who would be vested with extraordinary powers."

The person tapped to be this new, all-powerful commissioner was a federal judge from Chicago named Kenesaw Mountain Landis. "The only thing in anybody's mind now is to make baseball what the millions of fans throughout the United States want it to be," he said. A tough, shrewd, calculating, and grandiose man, Landis governed the game with a firm if discriminating hand until his death in 1944. Johnson did not fare as well. With his standing among baseball's ruling elite greatly diminished, he tried to hold on gamely as AL president over the next few seasons but was obliged to step down in 1927 due to declining health. He passed away three years later.

If Boston fans had been irritated by the Mays departure and their team's lackluster finish in 1919, they became positively enraged when word arrived the following January that Frazee had sold Babe Ruth to the Yankees for a then-record sum of $125,000. As the *Boston Post* editorialized, "A 45-rounder between the Crown Prince and the Kaiser on Bunker Hill would scarcely have raised any more disturbances among Boston sports followers." To be sure, Ruth's singular accomplishments in a Boston uniform belied the callous manner in which he had been dealt.

"Ruth was ninety percent of our club last year," said Royal Rooter Johnny Keenan. "It will be impossible to replace the strength Ruth gave the Sox. The Batterer is a wonderful player and the fact that he loves the game and plays with his all to win makes him a tremendous asset to a club. The Red Sox management will have an awful time filling the gap caused by his going." Boston Athletic Association president Edward E. Babb echoed these sentiments, claiming the deal was "a big mistake." "However," he added, "as baseball is handled today, it is not surprising to learn of startling things happening."

The *Boston Globe* was far less sanguine in its response. In an editorial titled "Athens of America," the paper speculated that it was possible that "unscholarly persons will rise and remark that the prevailing excitement concerning a man who merely made 29 home runs is unbecoming Boston's reputation as a center of learning." Nevertheless, such views had to be taken with a grain of salt. "If any assertion of the sort is made," the *Globe* maintained hyperbolically, "it will only indicate a lack of classical culture. Ancient Greece was both the intellectual and athletic center of the world. . . . Any Bostonian who feels sad on the subject of Mr. George H. Ruth may remember Athens and then give full vent to his grief in public."

Not everyone viewed the transaction as a total disaster. One thoughtful Cambridge fan said he admired Frazee's willingness to "incur the enmity of the fans," so long as his effort produced "a happy, winning team." Even the *Boston Herald*, which had printed mostly laudatory items about Ruth, warned that stars of his caliber were frequently "temperamental." "They often have to be handled with kid gloves. Frazee has carefully considered the Ruth angle and believes he has done the proper thing. Boston fans undoubtedly will be up in arms but they should reserve judgment until they see how it works out."

In explaining the move, Frazee informed the press he had little choice, given what he considered to be Ruth's poor attitude and lack of overall professionalism. "Had he been possessed of the right disposition, had he been willing to take orders and work for the good of the club like the other men on the team I would never have dared to let him go, for he has youth and strength, baseball intelligence and was a popular idol," he said. "But lately this idol has been shattered in the public estimation because of the way in which he has refused to respect his contract and his given word."

Frazee even denigrated the famed slugger's hitting ability, going so far as to say that Ruth's home-run blasts had been overrated. "How many games can you point out that he won single-handed and unaided last season? He won some, I will admit, but many a time it has been some other player on the team that contributed the deciding smash. Only Babe's long hit always got the credit. We finished in sixth place in spite of Babe and his 29 home runs," Frazee stated.

"This will bring out, I think, very clearly the fact that one star on a team doesn't make a winning ball club. Cleveland had the great Lajoie for years and couldn't win, Detroit had its Ty Cobb and Boston had its Ruth. A team of players working harmoniously together is always to be preferred to that possessing one star who hugs the limelight to himself," opined Frazee. "And that is what I am after—a team of steady, harmonious players. Harmony had departed when Ruth began to swell and I doubt if we could have kept out of the second division this year with Ruth in the lineup. After all, the baseball fans pay to see games won and championships achieved. They soon tire of circus attractions."

The "circus attraction" in question was not in good humor when he learned of Frazee's rambling ad hominem attack. "I have given my best," said Ruth from his off-season vacation retreat in California. "I have been with the Red Sox for six years and in that time we won three pennants. Not so bad? I am not a disturbing element. I have always played in the interest of the public and players and Frazee knows it."

As for his own estimation of Frazee, Ruth did not mince words. "He cares nothing about Boston people," he claimed. "Frazee is not good enough to own any ball club, especially one in Boston. It is not necessary for me to say he is unpopular, for that's a fact well known by anybody within the game. He has done more to hurt baseball in Boston than anyone who was ever connected with the game in that city. The Boston people are too good for him and it will be a blessing when he steps down."

In point of fact, Frazee had no intention of selling the Red Sox—at least in the short term. He enjoyed the game, which he likened to "show business," too much. Nevertheless, there were ominous signs that all was not well in his business empire. While the 1919 season had been a profitable one for the Boston honcho, he found himself on unexpectedly shaky financial ground once November came around. Joseph Lannin, the former Sox owner, began pressuring him to make good on an outstanding $250,000 note that Lannin had floated him for the purchase of the club in 1916. Frazee was unable to pay, however, as his bankbook had been stretched thin by his other far-flung theatrical enterprises. Indeed, his latest stage production, the three-act comedy *My Lady Friends*, was scheduled to open in New York City in early December. "Those are the only friends that son of a bitch has," one disenchanted Sox supporter quipped later.

If this wasn't bad enough, Frazee had to also contend with new salary demands from Ruth. Coming off the greatest season of his young career, the future "Sultan of Swat" announced he would play for nothing less than a $20,000 raise in 1920. Frazee could either give him the money he was looking for or he would retire from baseball, presumably to take up a second career as a film actor. Already he had signed a $10,000 contract to star in a six-reeler that was scheduled to begin shooting later that off-season. "Needless to say, Babe's strong face will add greatly to the picture," wrote one impressed journalist.

Frazee was in a real fix and he knew it. To avoid financial disaster, he entered into negotiations with Jacob Ruppert to sell Ruth, knowing full well the beer tycoon was the only owner in the game that could meet his steep asking price. To his credit, Ruppert knew a golden opportunity when he saw one. He thought the acquisition of Ruth would give New York fans "an aggressive, strong, and

Jake Ruppert, pictured here to the right of baseball commissioner Kenesaw Mountain Landis, systematically stripped the Red Sox of most of its talented players in the early 1920s and subsequently used them as a foundation for an even greater baseball dynasty. (Courtesy of the Library of Congress.)

balanced team that would be in all respects worthy of the league's greatest city." The details got quickly worked out. In exchange for Ruth, Frazee received $125,000 as well as a $300,000 personal loan, the existence of which both parties elected not to disclose publicly. The latter made perfect public relations sense, given that Frazee had put up Fenway Park as the security for the loan.

Bostonians no doubt would have been aghast at the knowledge of a rival league operator like Ruppert holding the mortgage to their beloved team's home ballpark. To Frazee, however, it represented a sound business move. He could discharge his debt to Lannin while still retaining control of the club. "I can't turn that down," he reportedly said.

Even so, the whole matter might have been rendered superfluous if Ruth had refused to go to New York. To avoid such an outcome, Ruppert had wisely dispatched Yankees manager Miller Huggins to California for the purpose of sounding out the unpredictable home-run champ.

"I know you've been a pretty wild boy in Boston, Babe, and if you come to New York it's got to be strictly business," Huggins intoned. Ruth didn't bat an eye. He informed Huggins that he would play to the utmost of his abilities for the Yankees, "or anybody else," he shrewdly added. "But listen," he said, "if I go to New York I'll want a lot more dough than the $10,000 Frazee paid me last year."

Now it was Huggins's turn to act nonplussed. "I'm coming to that," the diminutive former Cincinnati and St. Louis infielder told Ruth. "We know you've built yourself to the top. The Colonel [Ruppert was a ceremonial colonel in the New York National Guard] is a generous man and if you promise to behave yourself when you come to us, the Yankees will tear up your old Red Sox contract and make it $20,000."

Ruth saw no reason to dispute these terms. He officially became a Yankee and proceeded to demolish the league over the next two years, averaging a robust .370 and knocking in an aggregate 308 runs. In the long-ball department, Ruth was equally proficient. He swatted fifty-four homers in 1920 and added fifty-nine more the following season to easily surpass his 1919 record.

"I have seen hundreds of ballplayers at the plate," Paul Gallico of the *New York Daily News* observed later, "and none of them managed to convey the message of impending doom to the pitcher that Babe Ruth did with the cock of his head, the position of his legs and the gentle waving of the bat, feathered in his two big paws."

In putting on this impressive offensive display, Ruth inspired other hitters to do the same, thereby deemphasizing the "inside baseball" strategy of the bunt and the steal that devotees like Ty Cobb and John McGraw had embraced during the Deadball Era. The home run was king now, and the new practitioners were young up-and-coming sluggers like Rogers Hornsby, who connected for forty-two dingers in 1922. As a result, scoring collectively went through the roof.

"Before 1920 it was a rare year when more than two or three men in both leagues batted in 100 runs," notes historian Robert W. Creamer, "but in 1921 fifteen players did it, and the average for the 1920s was fourteen a year." Even the normally recalcitrant McGraw had to adjust to the changing times. "There is no use in sending men down on a long chance of stealing a bag when there is a better chance of the batter hitting one for two bases, or, maybe, out of the lot," the Giants manager said.

After "slumping" to thirty-five homers and a .315 batting average in 1922, Ruth rebounded the next year, going the distance forty-one times and hitting a career-best .393. "There is one thing that Babe can always be counted on to supply," St. Louis Browns pitcher Urban Shocker revealed at the time. "He gives the opposing pitcher a thrill no matter what happens. If you strike him out you get a very pleasurable thrill, as long as it lasts. If he hits you for a solid smash you get another kind of thrill; why do cowboys ride wild steers and risk their necks bucking broncos? It is a dangerous sport but it gives them a thrill, I suppose, to think they have conquered something which was strong and reckless and hard to handle."

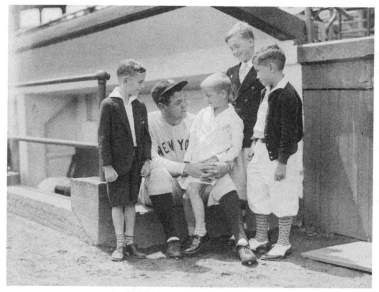

The Babe still accommodated young Boston fans with autographs when his powerful Yankee club came to Fenway Park. (Courtesy of the Boston Public Library Print Department, Sports Temples of Boston Collection.)

Not many pitchers could boast of having "conquered" Ruth in the 1920s. He was simply on too much of an offensive roll, hitting a total of 462 homers for the decade. In 1927, he set a new single-season home-run record with sixty blasts, which stood until 1961. "Sixty, count 'em, sixty!" Ruth exclaimed afterward. "Let's see some other son of a bitch match that!"

Through it all, he continued to find the time to amuse himself away from the ballpark. "All the lies about Ruth are true," Waite Hoyt said. Simply put, Ruth was the proverbial "life of the party," complete with a mischievous twinkle in his eye and an "anything goes" attitude. "He was a parade all by himself," wrote sports columnist Jimmy Cannon, "a burst of dazzle and jingle, Santa Claus drinking his whiskey straight and groaning with a bellyache caused by gluttony."

"You had to understand him like this," recalled teammate Joe Dugan. "He was an animal. No human being could have done the things he did and lived the way he did and been the ballplayer he was. Name any of them. Cobb? Speaker? Listen, I saw them all. I was there. There was never anybody close. When you figure all the things he did then you just have to remember he wasn't human. He was a god."

Ruth's extracurricular activities did not appear to interfere with the performance of the Yankees on the playing field, as they won six AL pennants and three World Series titles during this period. The Red Sox, alas, were a different story.

In the three seasons that followed Ruth's departure for New York, the Boston Red Sox failed to reach the .500 mark and finished an average of twenty-three games out of first place. Most of the blame for this dismal showing can be laid squarely at Frazee's feet. Still in need of cash to prop up his myriad theater interests, he peddled away a steady stream of stars and soon-to-be stars—players like Waite Hoyt, Wally Schang, Everett Scott, Joe Bush, and Sam Jones—to Ruppert's Yankees. Of course, by this time Frazee had given up any pretense of fielding a competitive squad.

As the estimable *Reach's Baseball Guide* reported in 1923, "Boston's last season reaped the fruits of four years' despoliation by the New York club, and for the second time in American League history this once great Boston team, now utterly discredited, fell into last place—with every prospect of remaining in that undesirable position indefinitely."

The final indignity came on April 18, 1923, when Frazee appeared as Ruppert's special guest of honor during the Opening Day ceremonies of the recently completed Yankee Stadium in the Bronx section of New York City. His Red Sox were the scheduled opposition that day and they obligingly went down in defeat, 4–1.

To add further insult to injury, Ruth supplied the game-winning home run for the Yankees with two men aboard in the fourth inning. Wrote one bemused witness, "The fans were on their feet yelling and waving and throwing scorecards and half-consumed frankfurters, bellowing unto high heaven that the Babe was the greatest man on earth, that the Babe was some kid, and that the Babe could have their last and bottom dollar, together with the mortgage on their house, their wives and furniture."

The ballpark became known as "the House That Ruth Built," but a more apt nickname might have been "the House That Frazee Built," given the amount of high-caliber talent the financially strapped Boston owner sent Ruppert over the years. "The Yankee dynasty of the twenties was three-quarters the Red Sox of a few years before," Harry Hooper said. "All Frazee wanted was the money. He was short of cash and sold the whole team down the river to keep his dirty nose above the water. What a way to end a wonderful club."

Frazee sold the club to an ownership group headed by former St. Louis Browns executive Robert Quinn in the middle of the 1923 season. Woefully underfinanced, Quinn could do nothing to ameliorate the team's already desperate situation. Boston finished last eight times during his ten-and-a-half-year reign, which ended mercifully when millionaire "sportsman" Thomas A. Yawkey purchased the club in 1933. "I've been quoted as saying that the big mistake of my career was when I left the Browns in 1923 to go to the Red Sox as president and part owner," Quinn said later. "I don't remember ever having said that, but perhaps it is true, the way things turned out."

Although Yawkey would pump a small fortune into the team, the Red Sox produced only three AL pennants (1946, 1967, and 1975) and zero World Series championships in his four-plus decades as owner. He was, however, able to pay off the mortgage note that Ruppert still held on Fenway Park. Only he paid for it a lot sooner than he had expected.

"I went to the Colonel [early in the 1933 baseball campaign] and told him I had already laid out a great deal of cash, and I wondered if he could carry the mortgage into the following year," Yawkey told the writer Henry Berry in 1974. "He said yes, he was delighted to have me in the league."

But Ruppert experienced an abrupt change of heart later in the season when Yawkey's Sox swept the Yankees at Fenway in five straight games. "The next morning my lawyer in New York called me to say it was a costly sweep," Yawkey said. "Ruppert's lawyer had just called, and they were demanding payment right now on the mortgage. Jake didn't like to lose five straight. So I sent the SOB . . . a check the next day."

When Yawkey died of leukemia in 1976, his widow, Jean Yawkey, became the team's principal owner. She had no better luck producing a championship either, although her 1986 squad came tantalizingly close during game 6 of that year's World Series against the New York Mets.

Up three games to two and leading the host Mets by two runs entering the bottom of the tenth inning at Shea Stadium, Boston seemed on the verge of closing things out when the first two New York batters were retired on fly balls. Then disaster struck. The Mets tied the game on three straight hits and a wild pitch by Boston reliever Bob Stanley.

Stanley hung tough, however, and got New York's Mookie Wilson to hit a grounder to teammate Bill Buckner at first. With shades of Fred Snodgrass from the 1912 World Series, the ball went inexplicably through Buckner's legs, allowing Mets base runner Ray Knight to score the winning run from second. Completely demoralized from the defeat, Boston could not mount a comeback in game 7, dropping the contest 8–5. "One fuckin' out," Sox manager John McNamara said later. "That's all we needed was one fuckin' out."

Such heartbreaking losses had led many to conclude that the franchise was cursed for having sold Babe Ruth to the Yankees, and "the Curse of the Bambino" was a widely held superstition among baseball fans. "Ruth never uttered any farewell curse; he knew opportunity when he saw it," newspaper columnist George Vecsey wrote. "But his departure cast a spell that festered in the crevices and eaves of Fenway Park."

All this talk of supernatural hexes finally ended when the Red Sox swept the St. Louis Cardinals in the 2004 World Series. Fittingly, Boston reached the Series after staging "the Greatest Comeback in Sports History" against the Yankees in the American League Championship Series.

Down 0–3 in games, Boston reeled off four consecutive victories, including two extra-inning triumphs, to take the pennant. "It's fate, destiny, all those things rolled into one," former Sox third baseman and 1986 World Series veteran Wade Boggs told sportswriter Dan Shaughnessy afterward. "I felt such a warming glow. . . . The big black cloud was lifted."

New Boston owner John Henry, the publicity-shy billionaire who had purchased the club from the Yawkey estate two years earlier, was typically more circumspect in his reaction. "It's just a remarkable season," he said.

Remarkable also describes what the Red Sox had managed to accomplish between 1912 and 1918. As for those principal cast members who helped make this baseball success story possible, some, like Ruth, went on to greater fame and glory, while others did not. Tris Speaker fell into the former category.

In 1920, Spoke led the Cleveland Indians to their first World Series championship as player-manager. He hit .388 on the season and continued to wow fans with his spectacular play in the outfield. More importantly, he provided a much-needed calming influence in the clubhouse when his close friend and teammate Ray Chapman was killed by Carl Mays's fastball on August 17.

"The boys had a tough time of it getting squared away following Chapman's death," he wrote. "It was the hardest battle I ever had in my life to overcome my grief, and all of the boys felt the same way about it. But we realized that all our tears and heartaches couldn't bring dear Ray back, and we just pulled ourselves together with that which was uppermost in Chappie's mind—the pennant and the world's championship—as our goal."

Speaker remained at the Cleveland helm until 1926, when he resigned in response to an allegation made by former Sox teammate Dutch Leonard that he had schemed with Ty Cobb and Smokey Joe Wood to "fix" a ballgame against Detroit in 1919. While Speaker

Tris Speaker would win another World Series in 1920 with Cleveland as player-manager. He would later join the Senators and Athletics before calling it a career after the 1928 season. (Courtesy of the Library of Congress.)

and his alleged co-conspirators were exonerated of the charge by Commissioner Kenesaw Mountain Landis, he never managed in the big leagues again. He ended his playing career with the Philadelphia Athletics in 1928, hitting a lowly .267 in sixty-four games.

In retirement, Speaker worked as a broadcaster and as a part-time coach with the Tribe in spring training. He also didn't hesitate to criticize emerging new stars like Yankee center fielder Joe DiMaggio for supposedly not measuring up to the players of his era. "*Him?* I could name fifteen better outfielders!" he scoffed. Elected to the Baseball Hall of Fame in 1937, Spoke would continue to offer his unvarnished opinions of the game until 1958, when he died of a heart attack while vacationing in Florida. He was seventy.

Bill Carrigan took a break from his active business career and returned to managing the Red Sox from 1927 to 1929. Unlike his previous stint in the dugout, this time around proved to be an unmitigated disaster. "I don't think my mother was particularly happy about his decision," Carrigan's daughter Beulah recalled. Bereft of anything resembling major league talent outside of promising young pitcher Red Ruffing, the club finished in last place with 103 losses his first year.

Things didn't improve over the next two seasons either, as Carrigan could not lift the Sox out of the cellar. Longing for the "good ole days," Carrigan complained that the ballplayers of the late 1920s had become too genteel in their approach to the game. "I'll take players who get arrested every night and win ball games two out of three afternoons to the best behaved second-division gang ever assembled," he said.

Disgusted, Carrigan went back to his hometown of Lewiston, Maine, where he became president of the People's Savings Bank. He thrived in his new position, although he earned a reputation for being something of a skinflint. Remembered one former business associate, "He didn't like to loan money out to people because there was always a chance that it wouldn't be paid back; therefore, the bank was investing very heavily in government securities, government bonds and so forth." The man who remains the only Boston manager to win back-to-back World Series titles died of heart failure in 1969 at age eighty-five.

Carl Mays had several more outstanding years left in his durable right pitching arm, including two twenty-win seasons for the Yankees. But he could never live down the fact that his fatal beaning of Cleveland's Ray Chapman in 1920 forever branded him a baseball pariah. "Mays should be strung up," declared one irate opponent. While this sentiment was shared by many both inside and outside the game, Mays always maintained his innocence.

"It's not my fault," he told the writer Jack Murphy in 1971. "Chapman was the fastest base runner in the league, he could fly. He liked to push the ball toward second or down the first base line and run. I had to guard against this, of course. I knew that Chapman had to shift his feet in order to get into position to push the ball. I saw him doing this—I was looking up at him because I was an underhanded

Ending his retirement from the sport, Bill Carrigan, pictured here with Washington Senators manager Bucky Harris, would come back to manage the Red Sox from 1927 to 1929. It was a huge mistake. His teams finished in the league basement each season. (Courtesy of the Library of Congress.)

pitcher, my hand almost scraped the ground—and I threw my fastball high and tight so he would pop up. Chapman ran into the ball. If he had stayed in the batter's box, it would have missed him by a foot."

Mays left the game in 1929, the owner of a lifetime 207–126 record. In his final years, he became embittered that a contemporary like Rube Marquard could make the Hall of Fame while he was consistently passed over. "Rube Marquard was a great pitcher and I'm glad he made it," he said. "But my record is so far superior to his that it makes me wonder. I guess the answer is they just don't like me." Mays died in 1971 at age seventy-nine following a brief illness.

Jack Barry went back to his roots when he retired from the pro ranks in 1919. He became coach of the Holy Cross baseball team and led the Crusaders to the 1952 NCAA championship. Overall, he compiled an impressive 616–150–6 record in his thirty-nine seasons with the club. Known as the "Knute Rockne" of college baseball, Barry also had a major hand in preparing twenty-five of his players for the big leagues, including star New York Giants shortstop John "Blondy" Ryan. Yet in doing so, he always made sure to stress the importance of earning a college education. Said Barry, "Even conceding the boy success, the life of a professional ball player is at best not long; in the old days five years in the majors was considered good. It is mighty comforting for a player to have a degree to fall back on when his playing days are done."

While he received several offers to manage again in the majors, he never gave serious thought to leaving Holy Cross. "Running a big league club is too much of a headache and your job is too insecure," Barry explained. "Besides I get a terrific thrill out of teaching the game to these young fellows and helping them find out whether or not they want to enter the professional sport." Barry succumbed to lung cancer at age seventy-three in 1961.

Harry Hooper held out for more money following the 1920 season and was summarily traded to the White Sox by Frazee. "I was glad to get away from that graveyard," he said. In his five years with Chicago, Hooper put up some fine offensive numbers, including three seasons over .300. But when he approached Chicago owner Charles Comiskey about a pay raise in 1926, the seventeen-year veteran was unceremoniously handed his release.

His playing career cut short, Hooper tried coaching college baseball for a time before finally finding his niche as a postmaster in Capitola, California, from 1933 to 1957. He continued to follow the game religiously and took special pleasure in watching star center fielder Willie Mays perform for the San Francisco Giants. "He's a throwback to the old days," he enthused.

In 1971 Hooper was selected by the Veteran's Committee for induction into the Hall of Fame. It was an honor long overdue for the greatest right fielder in Red Sox history. "I've always thought I had the credentials and records to be voted to the Hall of Fame," he said, "but now it has happened, it's a little hard to believe." He died three years later of an aneurysm at age eighty-seven.

Joseph Lannin met with a somewhat mysterious end. On May 15, 1928, the former bellhop turned real estate mogul plunged to his death from a ninth-floor window of a hotel he owned in Brooklyn, New York. There were no signs of foul play, and authorities on the scene were quick to rule out the possibility of suicide, as "indications were that Mr. Lannin, who had been troubled for six years with a heart [affliction], was seized with a sudden attack and fell over a balcony of the window as he sought air."

In the immediate years leading up to this tragic event, Lannin had kept himself busy in a number of business endeavors, including the ownership of Roosevelt Field, the departure point for aviator Charles Lindbergh's famed "New York to Paris" transatlantic flight in 1927. His estimated net worth at the time of his death was somewhere in the neighborhood of $7 million. But money was far from the thoughts of those who knew him best when word spread of his passing.

"He had his heart and soul in baseball when he owned the Red Sox," said Bill Carrigan. "As a matter of fact, he gave almost too much time and enthusiasm to his ball club in 1914, 1915, and 1916. . . . [He] never would have sold the team if he had not been told by physicians that he would have to get away from the excitement of baseball or shorten his life. He was as big a fan as any of the thousands who used to go to Fenway Park and see the Red Sox play." Lannin was sixty-seven.

Smokey Joe Wood's transition from the pitcher's mound to the outfield proved highly successful. Between 1918 and 1922, he hit .270 or better four times, including a career-best .366 for Cleveland in 1921. "It took nothing to play the outfield," he told the author Jack Lautier in 1982. "Catching a ball was easy. I had to work at becoming a better hitter. I choked up six or eight inches on the bat to get better balance. It takes a natural like Shoeless Joe Jackson to hold the bat at the end. When I was pitching, I held the bat that way. I tried to hit them a mile, like the boys do today, but now I had to hit to keep a job."

Wood hung up his spikes for good in 1923 when he accepted an offer to coach baseball at Yale University. "I grabbed that job in a minute because I wanted to be with my family more than I wanted to be just playing baseball," he said. In twenty seasons with the Bulldogs, he posted a 283–228–1 record to go with two Eastern Intercollegiate League championships in 1932 and 1937. This success notwithstanding, he never forgot his halcyon days with the Red Sox, especially the 1912 championship season. "That was the year Fenway Park opened, so you might say we got it off to a good start," he proudly stated.

However, like his old teammate Carl Mays, whom he didn't particularly care for personally, Wood became frustrated later in

Following his professional days, Smokey Joe Wood coached baseball at Yale University for twenty seasons. He also found the time to rub elbows with such all-time pitching greats as Cy Young, Lefty Grove, and Walter Johnson at this 1946 Old Timers Game at Fenway Park. (Courtesy of the Boston Public Library Print Department, Sports Temples of Boston Collection.)

life that his own substantial contributions to the game did not warrant enshrinement in Cooperstown. In large part, he believed this oversight was due to his name having been unjustly "tainted" in the earlier Dutch Leonard game-fixing controversy. But he mostly kept such thoughts to himself.

"I can go over my career till my dying day and come up with the same figures [a career 117–57 pitching mark and a .283 batting average]," he said in his last interview. "All I know is that there was no one faster than me. But I don't care about it. I had my day and it's over, and that's it." Wood passed away in a convalescent home at age ninety-five in 1985.

Ed Barrow had counted himself among the many in Beantown who were dumbfounded by the Babe Ruth sale. "You're going to ruin yourself and the Red Sox in Boston for a long time to come," he reportedly told Frazee at the time of the controversial deal.

When the first opportunity arose for him to leave the ball club, Barrow seized it, ironically becoming general manager of the Yankees. Under his stern leadership, the pinstripers became the most dominant team in baseball, winning ten AL pennants and seven World Series between 1920 and 1938. Yet he won no popularity contests with his players as he continually tried to lowball them in contract negotiations.

When superstar outfielder Joe DiMaggio once approached Barrow about a substantial salary increase in the late 1930s, he was abruptly told to rethink his position. Not even Lou Gehrig, the superlative slugger from Murderers Row fame, had ever made the kind of money DiMaggio was asking, Barrow explained. "Then Mr. Gehrig is a badly underpaid player," DiMaggio said.

In 1939, Barrow was promoted to club president and presided over three more world championship squads before finally stepping down in 1946. He was in increasingly poor health, and after more than a half-century in the game, he had little left to prove. "I guess I'd do it all over again," he once said of his life's work. Death claimed Barrow at age eighty-five in 1953.

Harry Frazee too experienced great success after parting ways with the Red Sox. In 1924, he produced the smash Broadway musical *No, No, Nanette*, which netted him over $2.5 million in earnings. However, the notoriety associated with his having earlier sold Babe Ruth to the Yankees dogged him to his grave and beyond. Indeed, the longtime sportswriter Frederick G. Lieb took acerbic delight in posthumously referring to him as "the evil genie."

Such extreme characterizations have always irked Frazee's descendents, who feel the former baseball magnate has been unfairly demonized. "With each retelling of the story, Frazee has become more a character of fiction and less a man of history," complained his grandson to a newspaper columnist in 2003. "He became the ultimate scapegoat for devoted [Boston] fans who have found the failures of the [Red Sox] franchise increasingly hard to swallow, and for a franchise that has never been eager to admit its own failures."

Still, there is no getting around the fact that after the 1918 championship season, Frazee drove the team into the ground through a series of one-sided deals with the Yankees. "Nothing is too good for the Boston fans," he once said. His dubious record as owner would suggest otherwise. Frazee died from Bright's disease at age forty-eight in 1929.

Duffy Lewis managed to stay active in the majors long after he had stopped chasing flyballs for a living. The former outfielder became the traveling secretary for the Boston and Milwaukee Braves from 1936 to 1961, and in this capacity he was afforded the opportunity of witnessing a young Henry Aaron turn heads in his first major league spring training camp in 1954. "I clearly remember one writer (I won't mention his name) saying that Henry would never make it, he couldn't hit enough," Lewis recalled. "Most of us, though, were convinced we were watching a future star. It took only a few months to convince that one writer, too."

Retired, Lewis took up residence in Salem, New Hampshire, where he passed the time frequenting a nearby racetrack and entertaining visitors with tales from his baseball past. He especially enjoyed telling the story of when he was once inserted into a contest as a pinch hitter for Babe Ruth. "It was in 1914 and I was on the bench nursing a bad ankle," he said. "Bill Carrigan, our manager, sent me up to pinch hit, although I could barely run. I got a hit, too."

Though he was overlooked for Hall of Fame induction, an omission that is admittedly egregious, Lewis was accorded the honor of throwing out the first pitch of the epochal game 6 of the 1975 World Series between the Red Sox and the Cincinnati Reds. Lewis died in 1979 at age ninety-one.

Larry Gardner did not have to languish in Philadelphia for very long. After hitting a respectable .285 in 1918, Connie Mack traded him to the Indians the following spring, where he got to play under his old teammate Tris Speaker. Now in his early thirties, a time when most ballplayers begin to think of hanging up the spikes, Gardner staged a career renaissance. He batted at or above the .300 mark for the next three seasons, including a career-best .319 in 1921. In 1920, he led the team in RBIs with 118 to help pace Cleveland to the pennant. His stellar contributions did not go unrecognized.

At a special White House reception for the Indians during the off-season, President Warren G. Harding made a special point of praising the third baseman. "I know you are a good player, young man, because way back in the early '80s I knew a player by that name. He was with Cleveland in the old National League and was a mighty good man," Harding said. Living up to his cheeky reputation, an unmoved Gardner responded, "That was just about the time I was breaking in."

When he retired from the game following the 1924 season, Gardner dabbled in a number of business ventures, including a Cape Cod cranberry company. Finding all of this personally unrewarding, he returned to his old college stomping grounds and served as University of Vermont head baseball coach from 1932 to 1952. Although his teams never possessed much talent, he was able to produce eleven winning seasons. "I guess he liked the team to win, but all I remember was how warm and human he was with his players," his son Larry Jr. said. Gardner died at age eighty-nine in 1976.

Babe Ruth became a cultural icon. Celebrated from coast to coast as the greatest hitter in baseball, the St. Mary's Industrial School product was easily the most recognizable figure in American society during the 1920s and 1930s. Remembered Yankee teammate Roger Peckinpaugh, "Ball players weren't the celebrities that they came to be later on, with a few exceptions, of course like Ty Cobb and Walter Johnson. But the Babe changed that. He changed everything, that guy. So many, many people became interested in baseball because of him. They would be drawing 1,500 a game in St. Louis. We'd go in there with the Babe and they'd be all over the ballpark; there would be mounted police riding the crowd back. Thousands and thousands of people coming out to see that one guy. Whatever the owners paid him, it wasn't enough."

Ruth himself was no wallflower when it came to cashing in on his celebrity status. He appeared in a number of movie shorts, toured the vaudeville circuit, and endorsed such household products as Barbasol shaving cream. After failing to come to contract terms with the Yankees following the 1934 season, Ruth allowed himself to be talked into playing a final year for the perennially awful Boston Braves. It was a major mistake. "During that 1935 Braves training season I was a big draw," Ruth later wrote. "People were curious to see how I looked in a National League uniform, but the harder I tried the worse I did. My old dogs just couldn't take it any longer. . . . It was a rotten feeling."

Ruth's disposition hardly improved when the Braves broke camp and began playing in games that counted. In the opening month of April, for instance, he collected only four hits and four RBIs. "He still had that marvelous swing, and what a wonderful follow-through," Braves infielder Elbie Fletcher later recalled. "But he was forty years old. He couldn't run, he couldn't bend down for a ball, and of course he couldn't hit the way he used to. It was sad watching those great skills fading away. To see it happening to Babe Ruth, to see Babe Ruth struggling on a ball field, well, that's when you realize we're all mortal and nothing lasts forever."

Ruth did experience one final moment of glory. On May 25, he faced Pittsburgh hurlers Red Lucas and Guy Bush and connected for three home runs and six RBIs in an 11–7 loss to the Pirates at Forbes Field. His third homer, the 714th and last of his illustrious career, cleared the roof of the right-field grandstand and traveled an estimated six hundred feet. "I never saw a ball hit so hard before or since," Bush claimed.

While he later admonished himself for not retiring "on top" after the game, Ruth stubbornly decided to soldier on for another week before calling it quits on June 2. His final Braves stat line read a .181 batting average with six homers and twelve RBIs in twenty-eight games. "It was pretty much of a nightmare," Ruth admitted.

His playing days over, Ruth earnestly explored the possibility of becoming a major league manager. But when he received little or no interest from other clubs, he reluctantly decided to abandon the idea. "I felt completely lost at first," he wrote of his plight. "I thought I'd wake up and find it was a bad dream, and when it became apparent that it wasn't a dream, I felt certain that the phone would ring and it would be the Yankees or some other big league team in search of me—telling me it was all a mistake. But the phone didn't ring."

Having wisely invested his baseball earnings, a financially secure Ruth elected to spend the bulk of his retirement hitting the links and participating in various charity events. Among the latter was a special wartime benefit exhibition with Walter Johnson at Yankee Stadium in 1942. Rusty and out of sorts, Ruth had difficulty connecting on Johnson's offerings. But on the Big Train's twenty-first and last pitch, he blasted a ferocious shot into the upper deck of the right-field grandstand. Noted one impressed biographer, "It landed a few feet foul, but Babe didn't let that bother him; he simply went into his familiar home run trot, smiling and tipping his cap and basking in thunderous applause all the way around the bases."

Making the celebrity rounds: Babe Ruth visits the White House in 1921. (Courtesy of the Library of Congress.)

In 1946, Ruth was diagnosed with nasopharyngeal cancer. Despite an aggressive treatment program of radiation, the ex-slugger could not overcome the disease. He died two years later at age fifty-three.

His departure triggered an avalanche of testimonials throughout the land. Perhaps none were as poignant and affecting as that of former Kentucky governor turned baseball commissioner A. B. "Happy" Chandler. "While his bat is forever stilled . . . the mighty Bambino will not be forgotten as long as baseball endures," he eulogized.

Indeed, Ruth was destined to live on in active memory, just like the Red Sox dynasty from the sun-drenched days of his youth.

BIBLIOGRAPHY

For research into Red Sox history, an extended examination of such newspapers and periodicals as the *Boston Daily Record*, *Boston Globe*, *Boston Post*, *Boston Journal*, *Boston Herald*, *New York Times*, *Lewiston Sun-Journal*, *Seattle Post-Intelligencer*, *Baseball Magazine*, *Sports Illustrated*, and the *Sporting News* proved extremely valuable, not to mention enlightening. In addition, the Baseball Hall of Fame's clipping files on J. J. Lannin, Bill Carrigan, Dutch Leonard, Ray Collins, Larry Gardner, Ernie Shore, Harry Hooper, Jake Stahl, Everett Scott, Tris Speaker, Joe Wood, Tilly Walker, Dave Shean, Heinie Wagner, Herb Pennock, Wally Schang, George Whiteman, Amos Strunk, Ed Barrow, Carl Mays, Stuffy McInnis, Fred Thomas, and Joe Bush yielded a virtual treasure trove of information. Old feature articles from such defunct publications as the *Sporting Life*, *Sport Magazine*, and *Saturday Evening Post* were especially useful. Ditto for the Bill Carrigan and Jack Barry holdings at the College of Holy Cross archives and the Michael McGreevey collection at the Boston Public Library.

Finally, the following books and materials also provided major sources of information for *When the Red Sox Ruled*.

Abrams, Roger I. *The First World Series and the Baseball Fanatics of 1903*. Boston: Northeastern University Press, 2003.

BIBLIOGRAPHY

Alexander, Charles C. *Our Game: An American Baseball History.* New York: Henry Holt, 1991.

———. *Spoke: A Biography of Tris Speaker.* Dallas: Southern Methodist University Press, 2007.

———. *Ty Cobb.* New York: Oxford University Press, 1984.

Anderson, Will. *The Lost New England Nine.* Bath, Me.: Anderson and Sons, 2003.

Angell, Roger. *Late Innings: A Baseball Companion.* New York: Simon and Schuster, 1982.

Appel, Marty. *Slide, Kelly, Slide: The Wild Life and Times of Mike "King" Kelly, Baseball's First Superstar.* Lanham, Md.: Scarecrow, 1999.

Barbrook, Alec. *God Save the Commonwealth: An Electoral History of Massachusetts.* Amherst: University of Massachusetts Press, 1973.

Bates, Leonard J. *The United States 1898–1928: Progressivism and a Society in Transition.* New York: McGraw-Hill, 1976.

Berry, Henry. *Boston Red Sox.* New York: Collier, 1975.

Borer, Michael Ian. *Faithful to Fenway: Believing in Boston, Baseball, and America's Most Beloved Ballpark.* New York: New York University Press, 2008.

Broeg, Bob. *Superstars of Baseball.* South Bend, Ind.: Diamond Communications, 1994.

Brother Gilbert, C.F.X. *Young Babe Ruth: His Early Life and Baseball Career from the Memoirs of a Xaverian Brother.* Jefferson, N.C.: McFarland, 1999.

Browning, Reed. *Cy Young: A Baseball Life.* Amherst: University of Massachusetts Press, 2000.

Caruso, Gary. *The Braves Encyclopedia.* Philadelphia: Temple University Press, 1995.

Clark, Ellery H. *Boston Red Sox 75th Anniversary History, 1901–1975.* Hicksville, N.Y.: Exposition, 1975.

Cooper, John Milton, Jr. *Pivotal Decades: The United States, 1900–26.* New York: Norton, 1990.

Creamer, Robert W. *Babe: The Legend Comes to Life.* New York: Simon and Schuster, 1992.

———. *Stengel, His Life and Times.* Lincoln: University of Nebraska Press, 2004.

Deford, Frank. *The Old Ball Game: How John McGraw, Christy Mathewson, and the New York Giants Created Modern Baseball.* New York: Grove, 2005.

Dewey, Donald, and Nicholas Acocella. *The Ball Clubs: Every Franchise, Past and Present, Officially Recognized by Major League Baseball.* New York: HarperCollins, 1993.

———. *The Biographical History of Baseball.* Chicago: Triumph, 2002.

Dickson, Paul. *Baseball's Greatest Quotations.* New York: HarperCollins, 1991.

Douskey, Franz. "Smoky Joe Wood's Last Interview." *National Pastime: A Review of Baseball History* 27 (2007): 69, 72.

Durant, John. *Highlights of the World Series.* New York: Hastings House, 1973.

Ferrell, Robert H. *American Diplomacy: A History.* New York: Norton, 1975.

Fetter, Henry D. *Taking on the Yankees: Winning and Losing in the Business of Baseball, 1903–2003.* New York: Norton, 2005.

Foulds, Alan E. *Boston's Ballparks and Arenas.* Boston: Northeastern University Press, 2005.

Frommer, Harvey, and Frederick J. Frommer. *Red Sox vs. Yankees: The Greatest Rivalry.* Champaign, Ill.: Sports Publishing, 2001.

Gay, Timothy M. *Tris Speaker: The Rough-and-Tumble Life of a Baseball Legend.* Lincoln: University of Nebraska Press, 2005.

Gentile, Derek. *The Complete Boston Red Sox: The Total Encyclopedia of the Team.* New York: Black Dog and Leventhal, 2004.

BIBLIOGRAPHY

Gershman, Michael. *Diamonds: The Evolution of the Ballpark*. Boston: Houghton Mifflin, 1993.

Gillette, Gary, Eric Enders, Stuart Shea, and Matthew Silverman. *Big League Ballparks: The Complete Illustrated History*. New York: Metro Books, 2009.

Golenbock, Peter. *Fenway: An Unexpurgated History of the Boston Red Sox*. New York: Putnam, 1992.

———. *Wrigleyville: A Magical Tour of the Chicago Cubs*. New York: St. Martin's, 1996.

Graham, Frank. *The New York Giants: An Informal History of a Great Baseball Club*. Carbondale: Southern Illinois University Press, 2002.

Halberstam, David. *Summer of '49*. New York: Avon, 1990.

Hofstadter, Richard, and Beatrice Hofstadter, eds. *Great Issues in American History: From Reconstruction to the Present Day, 1864–1981*. New York: Vintage, 1982.

Honig, Donald. *Baseball America: The Heroes of the Game and the Times of Their Glory*. New York: Macmillan, 1985.

———. *The Boston Red Sox: An Illustrated History*. New York: Prentice Hall, 1990.

———. *The October Heroes: Great World Series Games Remembered by the Men Who Played Them*. Lincoln: University of Nebraska Press, 1996.

Hough, John, Jr. *A Player for a Moment: Notes from Fenway Park*. San Diego: Harcourt Brace Jovanovich, 1988.

Hubbard, Donald. *The Red Sox before the Babe: Boston's Early Days in the American League, 1901–1914*. Jefferson, N.C.: McFarland, 2009.

Hynd, Noel. *The Giants of the Polo Grounds: The Glorious Times of Baseball's New York Giants*. Dallas: Taylor, 1995.

———. *Marquard and Seeley*. Hyannis, Mass.: Parnassus, 1996.

James, Bill. *The New Bill James Historical Baseball Abstract*. New York: Free Press, 2003.

James, Bill, and Rob Neyer. *The Neyer/James Guide to Pitchers: An Historical Compendium of Pitching, Pitchers, and Pitches.* New York: Fireside, 2004.

Jones, David. *Deadball Stars of the American League.* Dulles, Va.: Potomac, 2006.

Kaese, Harold. *The Boston Braves, 1871–1953.* Boston: Northeastern University Press, 2003.

Kavanagh, Jack, and Norman Macht. *Uncle Robbie.* Cleveland: Society for American Baseball Research, 1999.

Klapisch, Bob, and Pete Van Wieren. *The World Champion Braves: 125 Years of America's Team.* Atlanta: Turner, 1996.

Koppett, Leonard. *Koppett's Concise History of Major League Baseball.* New York: Da Capo, 2004.

Kuenster, John. *The Best of Baseball Digest.* Chicago: Ivan R. Dee, 2006.

Lautier, Jack. *Fenway Voices: From Smoky Joe to Rocket Roger.* Camden, Me.: Yankee Books, 1990.

Leuchtenburg, William E. *The Perils of Prosperity 1914–32.* Chicago: University of Chicago Press, 1993.

Leventhal, Josh. *The World Series: An Illustrated Encyclopedia of the Fall Classic.* New York: Black Dog and Leventhal, 2006.

Levitt, Daniel R. *Ed Barrow: The Bulldog Who Built the Yankees' First Dynasty.* Lincoln: University of Nebraska Press, 2008.

Lieb, Frederick G. *Baseball As I Have Known It.* New York: Coward McCann, 1977.

———. *The Boston Red Sox.* Carbondale: Southern Illinois University Press, 2003.

Linn, Ed. *The Great Rivalry: The Yankees and the Red Sox 1901–1990.* New York: Houghton Mifflin, 1991.

Lipsyte, Robert, and Peter Levine. *Idols of the Game: A Sporting History of the American Century.* Atlanta: Turner, 1995.

BIBLIOGRAPHY

Liss, Howard. *The Boston Red Sox: The Complete History*. New York: Simon and Schuster, 1982.

Littlefield, Bill, and Richard A. Johnson, eds. *Fall Classics: The Best Writing about the World Series' First 100 Years*. New York: Crown, 2003.

Lowenfish, Lee, and Tony Lupien. *The Imperfect Diamond: The Story of Baseball's Reserve System and the Men Who Fought to Change It*. New York: Stein and Day, 1980.

Lowry, Philip J. *Green Cathedrals: The Ultimate Celebration of Major League and Negro League Ballparks*. New York: Walker, 2006.

McSweeny, Bill. *The Impossible Dream: The Story of the Miracle Boston Red Sox*. New York: Coward McCann, 1968.

Meany, Tom. *Baseball's Greatest Players*. New York: Grosset and Dunlap, 1953.

Miller, Ernestine. *The Babe Book: Baseball's Greatest Legend Remembered*. Guilford, Conn.: Lyons, 2005.

Montville, Leigh. *The Big Bam: The Life and Times of Babe Ruth*. New York: Doubleday, 2006.

Nash, Peter J. *Boston's Royal Rooters*. Charleston, S.C.: Arcadia, 2005.

Nowlin, Bill, ed. *When Boston Still Had the Babe: The 1918 World Champion Red Sox*. Burlington, Mass.: Rounder, 2008.

Nowlin, Bill, and Jim Prime. *The Boston Red Sox World Series Encyclopedia*. Burlington, Mass.: Rounder, 2008.

O'Connor, Thomas H. *Bibles, Brahmins, and Bosses: A Short History of Boston*. Boston: Trustees of the Public Library, 1984.

———. *The Hub: Boston Past and Present*. Boston: Northeastern University Press, 2001.

Okkonen, Marc. *Baseball Uniforms of the 20th Century: The Official Major League Guide*. New York: Sterling, 1991.

Okrent, Daniel, and Harris Lewine, eds. *The Ultimate Baseball Book*. Boston: Houghton Mifflin, 1991.

Okrent, Daniel, and Steve Wulf. *Baseball Anecdotes*. New York: Oxford University Press, 1989.

Redmount, Robert S. *The Red Sox Encyclopedia*. Champaign, Ill.: Sports Publishing, 2002.

Reichler, Joseph L., ed. *The Baseball Encyclopedia: The Complete and Official Record of Major League Baseball*. New York: Macmillan, 1984.

Reisler, Jim. *Babe Ruth: Launching the Legend*. New York: McGraw-Hill, 2004.

————. *A Great Day in Cooperstown: The Improbable Birth of Baseball's Hall of Fame*. New York: Carroll and Graf, 2006.

Ritter, Lawrence S. *The Glory of Their Times: The Story of the Early Days of Baseball As Told by the Men Who Played It*. New York: William Morrow, 1984.

Ritter, Lawrence, and Mark Rucker. *The Babe: A Life in Pictures*. New York: Ticknor and Fields, 1988.

Robinson, Ray. *Matty: An American Hero*. New York: Oxford University Press, 1993.

Rosenburg, John M. *The Story of Baseball*. New York: Random House, 1964.

Rossi, John P. *The National Game: Baseball and American Culture*. Chicago: Ivan R. Dee, 2000.

Rucker, Mark, and Bernard M. Corbett. *The Boston Red Sox from Cy to the Kid*. Charleston, S.C.: Arcadia, 2002.

Ruth, Babe, as told to Bob Considine. *The Babe Ruth Story*. New York: Dutton, 1948.

Ruth, Claire Hodgson, with Bill Slocum. *The Babe and I*. Englewood Cliffs, N.J.: Prentice Hall, 1959.

Ryan, Bob. *When Boston Won the World Series*. Philadelphia: Running Press, 2002.

Scheinin, Richard. *Field of Screams: The Dark Underside of America's National Pastime*. New York: Norton, 1994.

Seib, Philip. *The Player: Christy Mathewson, Baseball, and the American Century.* New York: Da Capo, 2003.

Shaughnessy, Dan. *At Fenway: Dispatches from the Red Sox Nation.* New York: Crown, 1996.

———. *The Curse of the Bambino.* New York: Penguin, 1990.

———. *Fenway: A Biography in Words and Pictures.* Boston: Houghton Mifflin, 2000.

———. *Reversing the Curse: Inside the 2004 Boston Red Sox.* Boston: Houghton Mifflin, 2005.

Silverman, Jeff, ed. *Classic Baseball Stories.* Guilford, Conn.: Lyons, 2003.

Simon, Tom, ed. *Green Mountain Boys of Summer.* Shelburne, Vt.: New England Press, 2000.

Smith, Red. "Babe Ruth: One of a Kind." *Great Baseball Stories.* Avenel, N.J.: Crescent Books, 1994.

Snyder, John. *Red Sox Journal: Year by Year and Day by Day with the Boston Red Sox since 1901.* Cincinnati: Emmis, 2006.

Sowell, Mike. *The Pitch That Killed: The Story of Carl Mays, Ray Chapman, and the Pennant Race of 1920.* Chicago: Ivan R. Dee, 1989.

Sparks, Barry. *Frank "Home Run" Baker: Hall of Famer and World Series Hero.* Jefferson, N.C.: McFarland, 2006.

Stanton, Tom. *Ty and the Babe.* New York: St. Martin's, 2007.

Stout, Glenn. "Forever Fenway." *The Official 1987 Red Sox Yearbook.* Boston: Dunfey, 1987.

———, ed. *Impossible Dreams: A Red Sox Collection.* Boston: Houghton Mifflin, 2003.

Stout, Glenn, and Richard A. Johnson. *The Cubs: The Complete Story of Chicago Cubs Baseball.* Boston: Houghton Mifflin, 2007.

———. *The Dodgers: 120 Years of Dodgers Baseball.* Boston: Houghton Mifflin, 2004.

———. *Red Sox Century: 100 Years of Red Sox Baseball*. Boston: Houghton Mifflin, 2000.

———. *Yankees Century: 100 Years of New York Yankees Baseball*. Boston: Houghton Mifflin, 2002.

Stump, Al. *Cobb: A Biography*. Chapel Hill, N.C.: Algonquin, 1994.

Sullivan, Dean A., ed. *Early Innings: A Documentary History of Baseball, 1825–1900*. Lincoln: University of Nebraska Press, 1995.

———. *Middle Innings: A Documentary History of Baseball, 1900–1948*. Lincoln: University of Nebraska Press, 1998.

Sullivan, George. *The Picture History of the Boston Red Sox*. New York: Bobbs-Merrill, 1979.

Thorn, John, Pete Palmer, and David Reuther, eds. *Total Baseball*, second ed. New York: Warner, 1991.

Vaccaro, Mike. *Emperors and Idiots: The Hundred-Year Rivalry between the Yankees and Red Sox from the Very Beginning to the End of the Curse*. New York: Anchor, 2005.

Voigt, David Q. *America through Baseball*. Chicago: Nelson Hall, 1976.

Walton, Ed. *Red Sox Triumphs and Tragedies*. New York: Stein and Day, 1980.

———. *This Date in Boston Red Sox History*. New York: Stein and Day, 1978.

Ward, Geoffrey C., and Ken Burns. *Baseball: An Illustrated History*. New York: Knopf, 1994.

Waterman, Ty, and Mel Springer. *The Year the Red Sox Won the Series: A Chronicle of the 1918 Championship Season*. Boston: Northeastern University Press, 1999.

Weisberger, Bernard A. *When Chicago Ruled Baseball: The Cubs-White Sox World Series of 1906*. New York: William Morrow, 2006.

Whalen, Thomas J. *Kennedy versus Lodge: The 1952 Massachusetts Senate Race*. Boston: Northeastern University Press, 2000.

Winter, Jay, and Blaine Baggett. *The Great War and the Shaping of the 20th Century.* New York: Penguin, 1996.

Wood, Allan. *Babe Ruth and the 1918 Red Sox.* San Jose, Calif.: Writers Club Press, 2000.

Zingg, Paul J. *Harry Hooper: An American Baseball Life.* Champaign: University of Illinois Press, 1993.

Zinn, Paul G., and John G. Zinn. *The Major League Pennant Races of 1916: The Most Maddening Baseball Melee in History.* Jefferson, N.C.: McFarland, 2009.

INDEX